PHANTAS

By C Miller

M000036443

Introduction

Phantasmagoria:

- an exhibition of optical effects and illusions
- a constantly shifting complex succession of things seen or imagined
- a scene that constantly changes
- a bizarre or fantastic combination, collection, or assemblage

Introduction

Reclined in still, abandoned silence. Unclear as to whether these voices I hear are the mumblings of creativity, or if I'm slowly falling into insanity, unmindfully yielding to mental descent? Tip toeing back and forth between soundness and instability, the only words I understand are the ones I'm fortunate enough to write. Mental illness plagues. The battle between good and evil fatigues. What was I thinking? Have you ever wondered what goes on in somebody's mind? Is it possible that the words you're reading could be the rambling confessions of a delusional disorderly? Me. Statistics show that 1 of every 5 adults in the United States suffer from a form of mental illness. Could it be possible that the very words you're reading are the therapy preventing that one person from going over the deep end. Think about this, the promotional designers for products intend to communicate a subliminal message in every commercial right? Remember the advertisement for that popular drug awareness campaign starting with a cast iron skillet; the narration went, "this is drugs". It continued by cracking an egg into the same skillet, frying it furiously under extreme stove top heat, then finishing with, "this is your brain on drugs. Any questions?". A classic truth brilliantly communicated for the sake of illustrating dangers associated with drug use! The United Negro College Fund communicated a prevalent reality in saying, "a mind is a terrible thing to waste". Another all-time classic and arguably the most popular line of all time, "where's the beef?" The entire country adopted it as their favorite line for at least 2 years after it aired.

Introduction

That's what commercials aim for; shoot a pitch at the audience and hopefully it will catch fire and burn in their minds. Right? With that said, I imagine that you're primed for this incredibly profound truth. This is where I shoot my pitch to lure and lock you in! Share the wisdom of this all-to-helpful informative relevance but nope, nothing follows. Sorry, I just like commercials! "This is your brain on drugs!" Moral of the story is…. get ready for a bumpy ride! Therapy at its best! Don't judge me.

I'm C. Miller. Dad, Husband, Son, Friend, Preacher, Author, Teacher, Driver, Hustler, Business Owner, Motivational Speaker, so on and so on. I have a lifetime achievement award in the area of leaving task and endeavors undone. Unwilling to face the truth of insecurity and dislodged emotions, the saga continued. Over the years, I single-handedly managed to successfully fail when making life choices, choosing careers, holding to commitment and even honoring the sanctity of matrimony. The consequences negatively influenced the world around me at different stages of my life. I have failed at a lot of things. Not finishing is probably worse than failing because at least if failure was the reason most of the attempts didn't work, it's not in place because of the failing. Not finishing on the other hand, can be traced back to irresponsibility or faint heartedness. This book is my first big project and I am determined to finish it and spread it all over the world. At almost every point in my life, I have worn one of these hats with less than complete commitment.

Introduction

The only granule of character salvaged of all the things I've lived and experienced in life is an honest and loyal relationship with the lover I call Poetry. Poetry has never left my side since the day we met. "Poetry, it's easy to love me now. Would you love me if I was down, and out?" Yes, I belong to her and she belongs to me. For years, I've listened to random voices and memories echoing in my head for no reason. Sometimes the words would haunt me. The undeniable back and forth cadence calling between courage and fear. Other times the same voices would push me into sexually heightened moments of fantasy, leaving me embarrassed to share with people. My best friend taught me to write out my emotions in the 9th grade. Philadelphia High School, Philadelphia Mississippi, Mr. Myers chemistry class (I failed that class by the way), but I was so intrigued as well as relieved at the fact I had an outlet. I could write. I could take a blank piece of paper, stare into the empty lines of its premature possibilities, the set it aflame poetically. Ignite it and watch it burn in the secrets of my darkest emotional flames. Sounds cool? It is, always has been. The childhood pains of wondering why I had no mom or dad functioning in my life were probably my deepest resentments. Why they didn't care? Youthful teenage hormones. Loneliness of being different. The early discoveries of inappropriate intimacy with older women (I'm cool with that part now though). The difficulty meshing into an established school system where relationships had already been formed. The discomfort of growing up broke. We were so broke, but by the time I finished writing about the agony of falling asleep

Introduction

listening the lullabies of my squalling stomach growls, I felt better. Famished, yet able to cope by finding contentment in the distraction caused by focusing on my writing. I could write about anything, really get it off my chest! Stop right there…. "Get it Off Your CHEST!" I encourage you in the same manner Anton guided me using PM Dawn lyrics and childhood high school crushes suitably shaped to fit every testosterone filled teenagers imagination; as your friend, your brother and the dude that's doing the writing, find a way to "Get it Off Your CHEST!" Stifled emotions will kill you and while it may not always be possible to address all people involved, you must find a way. Understand? Of course. Write an angry letter to the person, an apology, a smoking hot love letter. Regardless of whether you give it to them or not, you expressed it. I'm not going into detail about all that because for now, the focus is poetry; however, there must be an outlet that enables you to ease pressures building from the bottled-up anxieties of life. Now, let's get back to the poetic beginnings…

So, I started writing, essentially motivated by my interest in girls that had taken off like a jet plane! That was the coolest thing to me. Girls were always so pretty and smelled good too. Hormones skyrocketed. Whatever people suspect young horny adolescent males do, my body was encouraging me to do that, and do a lot of it! The only problem, I wasn't an athlete. I was a timid chubby kid from Jackson Mississippi doing his best to adjust to the attitudes of my new surroundings. Every adjustment I attempted pushed me further out of the

Introduction

social circles of my peers and deeper into the solitary confinements of my thoughts that wound up dribbling all over the paper. The kids at Philadelphia High School didn't know me. I think I overshot my first impression intro many times and it didn't go well with the girls at all.

Wait, it's cool, turned out ok. Better than good in many ways because remember, I'm a writer. What's that supposed to mean? I'm glad you ask. Well for a writer, the only thing that matters is his writing. Once you master how to communicate exactly what to say, arresting the attention of the reader, manipulating their perception, you can do anything. Entice her tenderly curious sensualities and generate vibrational impulses she's never felt. You can stimulate her intellectually with burning thoughts to make her melt. Lick her cream-filled reality until she drips with savory illusions. If she reads intently enough, there's truly nothing she won't do. Nothing she cannot be, nothing she cannot see. Encourage her to spread the legs of her intellect and let me see. Let me investigate your thinking, paint impulses in your desire. Engulf you in flames of desire and watch you burn in the fire. See what I mean? I wrote love letter after love letter for classmates. I wrote essays. Whatever needed writing, I wrote it. Wrote it and loved what it made me feel. You know what? I still feel like that when I write. I wanted to share some with you in these following pages fashioned from years experiences. You'll recognize a variety of my life encounters in the pages. You will feel like you're moving thru the

Introduction

emotional stages alongside me, and just like I have felt countless numbers of times when reading the poems of fellow writers, you will probably be touched by the common emotions we may share in many of them. Some will be hurtful, some exciting, some will motivate you and others will be nasty! Downright freakiness! All I know to be is me and I am so happy that you're taking time to look inside my soul. I just want to share a little of my world with you. Before we go any further, let me tell you thank you for purchasing this book and taking time to read it. I appreciate your interest and support. So much love for you all.

Just like in high school, when I mentioned no particular activity or level of popularity identified me, that remains true today. I don't even think I want to be famous or "World Renown"!

I'm contently satisfied with myself, my family and my talents that it feels awesome just doing what I love! That's the foreseeable search we all pursue. Our individuality and significance! The freedom to be myself because can't nobody beat a person being themselves! In fact, I'm the best me that I know! Nobody can beat me being ME! Let me share a little of myself with you in the form of poetry, make rhythmic deposits into the beautiful places of your creative mind, draw on the broad canvas spread before you until the words cause light and depth to assimilate themselves in bleak, obscured darkness, giving new meaning to what you see. Can I be your poetry? Can I be your admired art? Plow into your thinking; you can see what I'm here being.

Introduction

Let me know you when I write. Can I be C. Miller? Can I be your poetry? Well, let's get started, shall we? Welcome the Phantasmagoria: Poetic Translations. Here begins a magically poetic moment in the life of one man.

Poetic Confessions

The Artist

As a Man Thinks

One day at a time's what I say to myself in an effort encouraging me to go on. Prayers weak and feeble, seemingly unheard, don't know how I've made it this long. I have a best friend, a close cousin and a fantastic brother, I love each one all the same. The more I listen to what we commonly suffer, we're existing inside the same vein. Emotional unsteadiness pours from our pain, poisoned and in need of transfusion. Strapped to the gurney of redundant instability, hopelessly reliving the same illusion. Its challenging being here, though I've been here before; I walk in the footprints of the fathers. They were just as rebellious, wrestled the same demons, giving in making their hard life even harder.

My family is on hold while I figure things out, that's hardly the right course man should take. Flip everyone off fondling in folly, the one I hurt is the only one that stayed. No way to describe the agony in her eyes, my actions trampled the pieces, she lay there and cried. The wife God gave me is the wife I mistreated, misused the affection she gave. After all the friends left, gold diggers had dipped, the same wife stayed right there and prayed. She's much stronger than me. I don't deserve her love. If I live 100 years, I can't repay it. She prays for me daily, loves me beyond measure, she's still hurting even when she don't say it. Emotional abuse hurts far worse than any punch a person could physically throw.

What's inside me is a darkness I may never outgrow, over the years hurt countless numbers of people. The figment standing

The Artist

before you is two desires in one body, you're witnessing the good and the evil. I'm coexistence, God in the flesh with the devil, two ends perfectly balanced on one scale. Visualize a winner on a long losing streak, a success that continues to fail. I'm the righteousness of Abel. I'm the sin of Babylon. I'm the Judas that's hungry for loot. I'm the hatred of the Klan, despising other races. I'm the black man praying they don't shoot me. I'm confused sexuality, not sure what to do after I'm touched in a way I shouldn't be. I'm the dislocated daddy, the cheating ass husband, I'm the poem for the poet to read. Low self-esteem flows in the arteries of the soul, cardiac arrest for all the others.

I'm the cancerous tumor in the back of her mind behind 4 abortions, I'm the black mother. I'm the protest testing the soundness of reason once the rally loses emotional momentum. Standing here before you in light skin lacking melanin, I'm the nigga that'll never fit in. White people hate me because I'm still black, but blacks say I ain't black enough. Dad didn't want me, he was married with children, mother left me, you can call me the mutt.

Either way, I'll be honest, not matter the case, we still must treat people fair. The Jericho stranger needing your helping hand wherever he is, you meet him there. Don't let your condition cause you to grow hateful, neglecting the needs all around you. Somebody sleeping under the bridge was looking for help, just before they died of hunger found you. The woman with the issue, the ying and the yang, the little light no matter how dark. Notwithstanding how good any of us may pretend, we're all the same, regardless who you are. Regardless your color, the money you have, regardless the people you know; There's a cost to be counted, a time to pay the piper and believe me there's an amount we all owe.

The Artist

There is no denying, in all the hustling and lying, there's one
thing I must confess. Whether in Mississippi, Texas or
Alabama, all mankind will take a test. Test of the mind to
calibrate the scales of integrity, ensure the weight is straight.
A test of the heart, would they do their part for the homeless
Lazarus at the gate. The beggar in the road on your way to
your business, while seeking to live your best life. I'm not sure
what your test is, may not even happen, but I want you to
know that it might. Don't steal, kill or lie, don't hide any
jealousy, honor your father and mother. The day's sure to
come when your test will be graded, He'll see how you treated
each other. Don't know what you heard, not sure what was
said, my life is not even my own. The words have been
written, calligraphy in the conscience, carved by the pen of
this poem

Morning Glory

Walked away from my morning,
Kissed her dawn goodbye.
Seduced by a lustful afternoon;
Afterwards ask myself "why"?

Walked away from my morning,
never bothered making her stay.
Never would feel another affection
that pushes the dark nights away.

Walked away from my morning,
craving the warmth of her glow.
Miss her radiance more in night's hour;
to bad she'll never know. Goodnight

The Artist

I AM

I am words. A series of collective collaborations drenched in gallons of experience. I am a communication so primitive your Neanderthal comprehension will not let people hear it.

I fall on the stale eardrums of the walking dead. Words from corrupt leaders will lead followers that shouldn't be led.

One day the words will cease. One day jammed between Facebook likes and changing trends, all the words you've ever heard, finally come to an end.

People will show up in the finest cheap suits and pretend they've always cared, but ask of them what words they heard then you will realize who was where!

The wheat will separate from the tares and all the world will see If they cannot live life by My words, then they have never heard of me. I am words

The Artist

It's Poetry

*Lustrous positioned systems, rhythmically driven
vantage points that inspire the systems rhythm. It's
poetry. Wittingly knowing where the implied intent is
going. Sagacious calls and shouts of indescribable
discontent. Emotional outburst that burst out from
within.*

*Death grins at the end of a life not worth living. Insanity
of each second sleeps in a night, unforgiving. Misfortune
rips the man in me apart in rage and anger. Women and
children view it, not considering imminent danger.
Recognizing decayed disbelief in dissertations;
annotated feelings still stapled to the paper. Confusing
moments of ramblings with incoherent display. Reading
it over hoping to understand he's saying.*

14

The Artist

Propose a Toast

Staring into the sky envisioning what it used to be, what it was. I saw it yesterday but never considered what it does. It came from last week's moments, gently in place while the brilliant sun rays accompany it warmly on my face. Tomorrow chased by yesterday but today won't run the race. Trapped like an animal; caged. Life's crippling evolution polluted at every stage.

Wonder what it will be? Wonder if all the blind wondering will even let me see? If I could recognize reflections, would I recognize me. I wonder if there's fear and are there any out here fearing it? Who we were whispers what we've been, but who we are just ain't hearing it.

Cheers to the valiant nobodies that nobody ever knew. Cheers to the empty dreams the sleepers never woke up to pursue. Cheers to all of life with its trips, slips and falls! Finally, cheers to the tipped-up glass never lifted to toast at all.

The Artist

Expectancy

*Two came into the office, but only one will leave. The
child that brought her so much joy, may be the reason
she grieves. His pale hand on her shoulder doing his best
to tell her easy. Only one of you will survive this birth,
I'm praying you don't leave me. Her or her child was
her only thought. Painfully indescribable
contemplations. Her husband stood there with tears in
his eyes, trying to be strong and not cry. To live in this
moment means living a lie, knowing one of them would
live, and one of them would die.*

*One of them would breathe and one of them would not.
One life would continue and one of them would stop. She
looked the doctor in the eyes and ask if he would leave.
"Please give my husband and I a moment", still clothed
in disbelief. "We need some time to talk; think about the
family we will not have. The pictures we will not take
and the laughs we will not laugh. Give us a moment to be
together as a family for one last time. Give me some time
to absorb the idea of my baby's life or mine." She burst
into tears and shook frantically, became undone on the
table. Her husband tried to hold her close, "Baby we
know God's able". "If God cares so much then why this
pain, why will one of us die?" "That question is not mine
to answer, so I won't even try. I will hold you and be
there for all of us until this pain subsides. I'll love
whoever lives for the sake of the one that died. I'll be a
good daddy or husband, whatever I'm blessed to be.
Because whatever God chooses to take away, He's still*

The Artist

*leaving someone for me! He's still Almighty and He
knows best even when it seems this bad. I love you and
our child even more because I love all that I've had."*

*She looked into his eyes and with a smile said "Honey,
you know you're right. I surrender myself to His will and
I'm going to sleep tonight. I hope He lets our baby live
because you're the best man ever. I've had my share of
loving you and I know our child could love you better.*

*Whatever comes, whatever is, then that's just what we
have. Never felt that someone I love this much would be
the reason I hurt so bad. Didn't cross my mind my
bundle of joy I'd never get to hold. To love one another,
we'll never know. This love I have for her, I can never
show.*

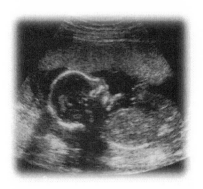

*Because of you and because of God, I face this hurt of
mine. I love you baby and I love this baby even if this is
my last time. Just hold my hand and pray with me
because this is the hardest thing I'll do. Not only
possibly losing my baby but knowing I may die and lose
you too."*

The Artist

He remained quiet. Water drops filled his eyes, it felt like he was dying. He was doing his best to hold back his tears, but he burst into crying. His words were choppy and slurred together while he huffed to catch his breath. It just became so surreal that he was losing all he had left. Either his wife or child would die at birth, either way would kill him. Being strong for him and her, both ways were killing him. He's standing here being strong for her. Strong for who they'll be and strong for who they were. He's standing there a broken man having done all he could to do. All he wanted was to love his family, now that's what he's about lose.

The Artist

The only difference in Hershey Kisses and Reese's is the flavor on the inside. The one is what it appears to be through and through while the other has a flavor inside that distinguishes it. For the longest I thought it was appropriate to mask the inner me for the sake of blending in, the more I attempted to blend, the more I didn't fit in. I could really go for a Reese's Peanut Butter cup right about now!! Calm down, it's two in the pack, I'll share with you. Anyway, the point I'm trying to make is that it's ok to be a little different. Not weird, hiding in the bushes, stalker like different, but individuality type different. Differences signify significance. Society puts a pressure on us that's unreasonable and unfair. Weight requirements, expectations to have children by a certain age, to go to college, to wear certain styles and trends; but what if none of that suits you? It is imperative that you, even while you're reading this now, search through the catalogue of your heart to determine what you want your life to be. Plan it out and begin sharpening yourself for that position and role. Live it out. Find it, learn it, then be it!! Live it!

****Boost: It's alright to not be accepted. To not be liked. To not have your ideas approved by the masses. You're you, enough said. Good Mantra is "I am enough. I have enough. I do enough"****

The Artist

Blurry revelations show me a person that can't be.

A proud unwilling imitation of a realness he believes.

False misrepresentation that only fill the eyes that see

Inside he hides a truth that he's never attempted to be.

Not willing to pay the cost because this freedom is not cheap

Wandering around lost pretending to have all he needs

Alone and incomplete he walks around in broken pieces.

Choosing to live imprisoned, while truth wait to set free.

The Artist

School Days

Chubby little kid picked on today, he fights to hold back tears. School's his only chore, his worse regret, damn he hates it here. The kids are so mean, make fun of him daily. Grandmother's no help, she says pray, but nobody can save me.

Books knocked out his hands, he's pushed to the ground.
First thought's, just stay down till nobody's around.
Second thoughts to fight back but it's so many kids,
He remembers how they all hit him the last time he did.

He was taught to be kind, who was teaching them?
Teachers ask if he's ok but there's no reaching him.

He would love to just restart the day or maybe run away
Even in bed at night the mean kids won't go away.
Nobody cares and he's giving up trying.
Playing with suicidal ideas, thinking about dying.

Nobody cares he's feeling scared or what he may have been thru. Nobody cares until his fears purchase his first pistol. Nobody cares, nobody hears, nobody can even see, Then he decides today's the last day the bully's bullying me

The Artist
What Happened

What happened to the other you? The one with big dreams, expectations of owning things and going different places; now you're here trapped between time and empty spaces, staring into untrustworthy eyes. The lovers that said they'd be true and made you fall in love with lies. Forced you to believe in them, do things you never thought you'd do. After all the questions life ask you, I asked "what happened to the other you?"

The person you were before the suffering? The girl that lived and laughed believing she would never feel pain. The wife who forgave her husband and he up and left again! The player that tore his Achilles and never made it to the league; made it thru recovery but never quite got on his feet. He never even knew. The NFL was the goal so now what does he do? Now who are these people supposed be. Or maybe they're somewhere writing this poem and one of those three is me?

Dropped out once his girl took the pregnancy test, gotta be a good dad; Better than mine no doubt, its sad good dads earn so much less for the family struggling as a high school dropout. Still can't stop now because that's what suckas do. After child support I got 232 dollars left to feed the other 2. Did I mention I had more kids?

Did I mention life can arrest your drive and suffocate your clearest vision? Did I mention I'm giving up on life and the voices in my head are making me listen? Suicidal tendencies, hoping my next breath will be my last. Baby momma talks so bad to me, kids don't respect their dad. Lost myself, own identity I can barely recognize. The imposter impersonating me prefers the truth but lives the lie.

22

The Artist

Balled up in a corner, living life from day to day. Uncertain. Despondent. Not knowing what he should do. A man that started with good intentions, now sitting here listening to some fat dude. One question sticks out, what happened to you?

The Artist
Life Fades Away

My purpose was on purpose, didn't match
the conception. Not perfect, I heard it
doesn't ask for perfection. But I'm certain
it's worth it, so I'm working & working,
still smiling but inside ya boyz hurting
and hurting. Built for the burden.
Behavior still inciting the curses,
inflicting the hurt. Instead of healing,
tickling nurses. I pay a price for sin that I
ain't got in my purse. Losing my soul in
efforts to gain material worth. Grass
withers, flower fades away and so does
the earth.

Oh yes, I'm the Great Pretender. Pretend
with the Creator so I have no defender.
I'm surrendered. Forgive me. Use me as
You will.

Said a prayer to God today and I'm
hoping He heard it. My body's a living
sacrifice, reasonable service. Best things
in life are free, complimentary version.
Wanna be great? Greatness comes from
humbling service. Sometimes mumble
when I'm crumbling so humble ya
servant. Too many blessings to number,
certain I don't deserve it. Still grateful for
Your mercies because it could've been
worse

The Artist
More to the King

Justified individuality held prisoner to expectations. The world you're running from still pushes you into place.

Pushes and suppresses your ambitions and expressions; nevertheless, don't let it hinder you, let it be a lesson.

Let this teach you. What's inside of you intimidates, do what others are afraid to do. Let it be your guiding thought, but not prevent you from being you.

It can't prevent me from being free in a world filled with prejudice thinking. It will not stop my ship from sailing, damn sure can't make it sink.

You must don the mantle of resilience and be hardened by the pain. Use courage to change what you can, serenity to accept what you can't change.

Nobody hears your music, so they can't sing the songs you sing. There's more to it than wearing the crown when it comes to being the King

The Artist

Lovemaking

*Always about more than love making whenever you cross my mind.
Climatic shifts, seasonal changes and the way you change with
time. Imagined what you would be if love was to die for and we
were dying? Imagined the happiest moment in life and you were
standing there crying. I imagined the truth of loving you but Leos
always lying so I cease to imagine anything.*

*No more land of make believe. No making mental imageries of a
'you' I cannot see. Close my eyes and find you in my heart, that's
where you'll always be.*

You're everything to me

The Artist

A Good Man

*Someone asked, "Where are all the good men at?". I ask
myself if I'm one. Wondered if my sons will struggle with the
things inside me left undone?*

*I wondered if God examined my life today, what would He
see? I wonder if He was to show me myself, could I tolerate
looking at me? Couldn't help but question decisions I've
made, they've influenced so many lives. Found myself face to
face with the truth, after having affairs with so many lies.*

*A past participle of painful preparations. Incarcerated
freedoms existing apart from reparations. Shackled to the
moment, locked in contemplation still wondering. Overheard
a question that left me here pondering. "Where are all the
good men at?"*

*Owning my transgressions. Resumé congested with heartless
irresolution, choosing to learn the lesson. Fumbling through
the pieces, choosing to reconnect em. Still staring at
consequences. The wage of sin is death. Understand me, I'm
dying more and more with every breath.*

*Writing out the vision. Focused and determined, don't scuffle
with indecision. Answering my own questions, responding
with interventions. Goals to win the title, don't take honorable
mention. Why give up my inheritance just to get a pension?
Why trade in the roots of life just to get extensions?*

*How could we hear this question and not take on the task?
Why play the Jim Carey part while you're out here wearing
the mask? How is this not a challenge, this question that she
asks? How could this not awaken a man that's tired of taking
naps? The summon was not for answers, the response should*

The Artist

be an act. A behavior if you will, so they won't have to ask. "Where are all the good men at?"

The Artist

*The troubling task,
toil and labor in the
heat of summer's
core. Turn more dirt
over, turn more dirt
over   while
wondering what it's
for.   Keep   digging*

*Driving   and
chopping   into
the stiff packed
ground   hoping
to   make   it
ready; back and
forth   between
shovel and hoe,
tilling the soil to
make new grass
grow.*

The Artist

*Suddenly a glimmer of bright tender sparkle. Look
closer, closer still. Surely a candy wrapper or some
other trash I see, a closer look still not knowing exactly
what this could be.*

*Rake a little
more in the dirt
piles to pull this
shiny thing
loose, reach to
grasp it
chuckling a
little, obviously
amused.*

*"I'll be damned" the
gardener said with a
grin fitted and styled on
his face. For certain
this isn't a chunk of
gold found in this dirty
place.*

*I'm sure this is
not the place for
treasure, but for*

The Artist

*the   hardest
chore of work;
yet I'm standing
here with this
bright   golden
nugget   that
leaped out from
the dirt.*

*I'm   standing   here
wondering what God
has done in giving this
thing to me. Should I
dig more or retire for
the   day   considering
this work complete.*

*The work I have
done has paid
for itself and
made all the
efforts
worthwhile.   I
could lay back
and retire for
the rest of the
day, admire my
findings with a
smile.*

The Artist

*Then thought for a
second and began to
recollect on the stories
he'd always read. How
people grow lazy after
yielding increase, he
decided his day was not
yet complete. Consider
the ant thou sluggard.
The tortoise and the
hare. The ant and the
grasshopper's
childhood lesson,
wisdom everywhere.*

*His desire was
not gold but
planting for
growth, back to
the tilling at
hand. If God
gave him one
nugget for his
one day of work,
how much more*

The Artist

would He give
him for staying?

With a smile and strong
focus, he dived right
back in to finish the
work he had started.
The race can't be won
by the people who quit
and cannot be ran by
half-hearted.

The writer learned something while this digger was
digging. He was not a gold-digger, he was just making a
living

So on with this
writing, on with your
work; let the nuggets
abound in the
blessing. Relentless
effort, be the best of
the best, let the work
of this farmer be
your lesson. Do all
to His glory while

The Artist

you fight the good
fight, with diligence
of heart and with all
your might. Labor
and strive by day
and by night, gold's
not your quest, you
came here to write

The Artist

Off Limits

You're not supposed to be here. There's a "do not enter" sign on my heart, we don't allow anybody near. Never had to say it plainly, you've forced me to be clear.

You're moving into an unauthorized space! The last person to come inside was lost without a trace. I love my lonely existence and the trust I have for me. Love the fact I can't be hurt protecting the parts you cannot see. Please leave. I'm protecting a heart that won't bleed from the love I don't need. Surely you have ulterior motive. Others told me they loved me until it was time to show it. Just leave!

Don't look at my fear or tamper with this weakness. Don't make me whimper words in silence when my heart doesn't feel like speaking. Don't resuscitate this hemorrhaging heart should it ever cease beating. Don't attempt to mend my soul when you don't have all the pieces. Don't! Don't! Just Don't! Leave now, Just Go! Don't you talk to me about healing when you can't understand my wounds. Don't talk of being born again except you fit me in the womb. Don't suggest I find a bride; I am not fit to be a groom. Life abundantly is not worth living, I look forward to the tomb. Not that I don't want to heal, I'm too embarrassed to remove the cover. Easy to say you love me now, but can you love the unlovable lover?

Can you tolerate what I've become in compensating for time? Would you condemn me in my only truth once I get tired of lying? Once God brings me back to life, will you

The Artist

remind me of when I was dying? A man is not supposed to cry, will you laugh once I start crying.

I'm crying on the inside. The tears fall relentlessly, yet I'm still a man. Yes indeed, I'm a mess but I do the best I can. He says He has a plan for me, but I don't know the plan. Now you've showed up wanting to walk with me through the plains of this weary land. You're in the unauthorized space called the broken heart of suffering man. Please leave.

Words are the single most influential means of energy available to humanity. By the words of your mouth you will live or die. By words the worlds were framed, communicated in continuity and pressed into the fabric of every societal make up. To sum it up, we recognize that we are only words. Once they're spoken, they can't be taken back. Now in a few more pages this poetry will take on a mind of its own, leaving you to absorb many personalities. I have thirteen different people living in my head and while I do my best to keep them at bay, they all have something to say. If you think I'm crazy, you're probably right! My only reply would be, give the other 12 a chance and don't let the one speaking now discourage you. That's number 4, he has an unusual sense of humor. You're so beautiful to me. Alright, enough of this small talk…. let's have some fun! Here's some poetry!

The Artist
Exhale

Writing is the exhaling of emotions. The very breath of my affection, feelings respired in pen stroke. Gasping to exist, persistently pressing against the pressure. Inscribing experiences attempting to hold it together. A time to say whatever, be whatever I choose to be. Catch my breath from life, take a break and just breathe. Breathe

Outside My Window

Staring out the window imagining places I'd rather be. Rather be out there with you, rather have you here with me. Rather feel the brilliant sun than be trapped inside these doors; break insanity's grip, brutalizing routines from before.

Staring out the window, imagining places I can never be. I can never be there for you and you can never be here with me. Connect the dots of creativity for a picture we cannot see. Painted pictures in my memory, still can't picture you with me. We can never be.

I'm just staring out the window....

The Artist

Anxiety is my closest friend. We've been together so long, we really know each other. I've held it in my bosom like she was the side piece of relief that caused dissention between me and my lover. I've grown to love her. I've learned that what I am is never good enough. I've learned that if people accept you for who you are it's only until you're not enough. **Make your own choices, make decisions for yourself and you will find that the same people that claim to "love you so much", will be the ones that up and left.**

Guilty by association. Associated with judgmental prejudices that never accepted me anyway. I live a life of loneliness and exclusion. The misfit that missed the fitting session yet still wants to fit into places that teach the sickest lessons. The people that care for me the least haunt my mind when we disagree because they always wind up leaving me. Wonder if it'll ever cease. Will I ever know the privilege of community or destined to live life as this lonely me?

Destined to be all I need. I'm nothing more. Mom and Dad didn't want me, I wonder what they had me for. Nothing from nothing leaves nothing. I wonder if God even cares. I wonder if all the praying's futile, I wonder if He's even there. Donned in dreadful dissatisfaction disillusioned by demented despair. In my mind's a holocaust, Hiroshima everywhere. Dead bodies and blood stains, I'm stepping over corpses. Stomping into my darkness and leaving behind my nothing more. Leaving children plagued emotionally that I didn't do

The Artist

nothing for. I've made them feel the pain of my inadequacy and now I'm struggling to help them find their way. We sit at the tables for dinner and don't know what to say. I look into their eyes and I know they want some answers. Emotional bankruptcy interrupts me whenever I attempt an answer. My response is sore jilted, filled with guiltiness and hurt. I humble myself stumbling being the dad they deserve. Standing out like a sore thumb, circles getting smaller. Writing's laced with hopelessness; seems I've lost all hope for this.

Scrolled through my contacts with nobody to contact. Nobody to reach out to because nobody even knows. No family to accept me, nowhere to even go. Everybody's busy pissing in their own dilemmas until they decide to piss in my house, then they give me their agenda. Everybody calls once their pressures comes to life, trouble with their children, jobs, money, house and wife. Trouble standing adversity, cowards and counterfeits. I missed the class of fitting in but manhood's the class they missed. They have issues, they call me with the list, I'm suppose I'm a good listener because all I do is listen. Holding the phone wishing the signal would be lost. They'd have someone that they needed then who somehow dropped the call. I think about the times I never was good enough it seemed. I think of how when shit hits the fan, they somehow call on me. I think of all the jokes they had about the writing and the vision. The ones that said it'll never work, thought I'd abort the mission. Well here I am still writing, the lonely the misfit with a wish. Still fighting, still going on. Wanting to fit in but still alone

ARTWORK

The Artist

Grand works of conception brood from daring naked endeavors to express one's true essence for all the world to see. Painters paint pictures that become things that couldn't be. They become.

Words directly pointed break the bones of the double jointed! Gifted abilities fall on calloused receptions of the unwanted but still we want what we can't have. Life has a funny way of its own, too bad we can't laugh.

Encouraged to move from an emancipated past, seems I'm in a rut. Trapped emotionally while life slow motions me, damn I feel stuck. Out of luck. Unable to move from the place we were because we're no longer there. Lost souls are not sure where they are, our peace is everywhere

Jigsaw society doesn't make sense, no one sees the bigger picture. Primitive portrayal of a strong black man in every episode, he's still a Nigga. Except there's anger, aggression and strife, this black man grows even madder. The song writers' portrayal of who he is in his home, but this black man still does not matter.

Prejudice still exist, probably always will; soon as we finish "Kum By Yah", prejudice is prejudice still. It's not a matter of changing others no matter how much we march or fuss. The change comes after seeing the bigger picture and change the picture of the "Nigga" in us

The Artist
California Love

Across the country life goes on,
and California's ablaze.
There's road rage on the
way to work, bills gotta be paid.

One city's smothered in smoke and ash,
the rest just keep on going.
Fire leaving thousands homeless
and the whole world's not knowing.

Government locked down senselessly,
focused on hopes to build a wall.
If a wall was built round the fire that way,
we probably could have saved L.A.

Not knowing or not caring
about the furious flames of heat.
Suppose we all take the same mindset,
"long as it's not me".

As long as my home's not in peril
and my kids are safe and sound.
Maybe someone will take the same
attitude when your city's burning down

The Artist

Regret

Sitting, thinking about what life could be. Staring out the window contemplating life for me. What do I see? Clouds folded, blues skies drifting free. Imagination holds every dream ever dreamed.

"What do I want to be when I grow up?" I don't remember that question being ask when I was young. I don't remember preparing to do the things I've done. I'm just here. Taking deep breaths like they're my last, draped and clothed in fear. Still afraid and alone. Living life to love those around me but still struggling on my own. Still notations in my phone that reflect the inner me. Sitting here sipping coffee face to face with the inner me.

Consequences of bad decisions being labeled "the enemy" but it's just life. Spent a whole vacation laughing and talking with my wife but ends this way. Best friend and his wife don't even have words to say. Kids self-sufficient and better off when we're away. Asking God to guide my steps but He's been silent with nothing to say. Sounds like mumbling when I pray, stumbling every day. Pridefully humbling myself knowing humble is the way.

The silence is killing me. Asylums with soundproof walls imprison me. Feeling guilty and unworthy even though she's forgiven me, but I died when I hurt her, there's no forgiveness for what's not living.

I want to be a daddy to the children I disappointed. I want to be the man of God that He chose and anointed. I want to be a good son to parents I've never known. I

42

The Artist

want to be a good brother to brothers I call my own. Some call me uncle and others say I'm their cousin and me, I'm trying to make up for all the things I ever wasn't. All the things I've never said and the hugs I never gave. All the time I wasted making up for time I never made. The costly mistakes made and still paying the price, still seeking the Christ, still fighting the fight. Just leave me be. Just let me die, living every day as a man that never understood why.

The Artist

Shhhhhh

Wait....Listen. You hear that? Shhhhh
The tender whisper of the heart's instructions, begging
for you to be more. Begging for power to come forth,
stand in strength and might! Imploring you to exhaust
yourself, don't you go out without a fight. Shhhhhh....you
hear that?

Did you learn from your last heartbreak? Did you take
heed to the signs? Did you set some immoveable
boundaries and they best not cross the line? What
happened to your existence? What happened to your
truth? How could you live in the depths of mediocrity,
how dare you not be you! How dare you not exhibit the
character of every forefathers' labor. How dare you fall
for these impressionable fallacies, and not do the things
you're able!

Not dreams the dreams of King, by any means like
Malcolm! Not climb the mountain like Moses, embrace
the priesthood as Aaron. Not come out from among them
choosing to live rather than die. If you hear the echoes
weeping, will you wipe tears from wisdom's eyes?
Wisdom cries aloud, only those with ears to hear can
listen. Turn reality TV off and reality on because there's
something we're missing. Shhhhhh

The Artist
Steal Still Time

I'm trapped. Caught in a web of delusional daydreaming.
Standing still in time, wishing time would stand still
while there's still time. Let's steal time. Unconscious of
my today. Lost, drifting in and out of illogically
transforming patterns. Sensibly reasoning and wondering
"what does logic even matter?" A desire so intriguing,
makes wanting you want you badder. Oh, excuse me
"more bad!" My bad but I'm subject to the subject,
you're in my mind like CAT scans, repositioning the
prepositions, a change of mind will change the positions.
Truthfully speaking, I lie to myself, denying it is what it
is, silencing the lies in brutal contemplation figuring it is
what it is.

If time could stand still, paralyzing polarity, I'd break all
the clocks and take you anywhere with me if time could
stand still. Still, so we could get lost in that moment; that
moment of stilled time. Yet I'm here helplessly
daydreaming in my real mind, hoping there's still time.
Whisper to you reminding you the ways, methods and
means. There's always a way no matter how hard it
seems. You can always dream just determine to be your
own dream come true, then daydream of me while I
daydream of you. There's still time; especially in these
arms of mine if time could stand still.

Look in your eyes and kiss you slow to breathe life in
you again. Blow on the smoldering embers, one day soon
you'll fight again. I see you full of fire. Energy in the
inner me burning with desire. I see the sparkle in your
eye, bigger than you could ever dream. You'll see it too

The Artist

real soon, please promise me this, when you recognize it
happening, you'll say just what it is. Make real time
stand still, steal time while there's still time...

Trapped

It's one thing to fall while trying, efforts to be what you're destined to be. Collapse briefly, moments of dying, heave a sigh of humility. Don't stop!

Going half past your passion, dashing fast then almost crashing – seeing visions of your past and what you wanted is what you had. Publicly humiliated by your own indiscretions. Struggling to hold your head up, taking steps with no direction! What didn't kill you was a lesson. Slow if you must but don't you stop!

Heartbreaks from disappointment. Dreams haunt and talk taunts the noble King or Queen. Hallucinations spring from still birthed dreams.

Still there's a pulse, a heartbeat of evidence. Since there's life, there's hope and chance. Don't succumb to circumstance. Don't' give up, take one more lap! Out of all my fear and anxiety, the memories of failures that reside in me, I'm still here. I'm still strong. Strong enough to last after all my strength seems sapped. My greatest fear is to die with potential behind walls of uncertainty...trapped.

The Artist

Circles

Teardrops fall
silently in the ocean,
only the one crying will
know. Break up
repeatedly, screaming
"just leave!", but stay;
too unhappy to go

When the truth is told in
secret of heart, only the
one lying will know.
Now we're too old. My
happily ever after
soulmate makes me cry
in my soul

Only the one healing
can cope with the
feelings and hopefully
make it one day make
sense.

Perhaps they can figure
out just
where they're going, to
never end up where
they've been

The Artist
Writer's Block

Writers block is labeled as condition. A condition in which the writer is unable to come up with fresh ideas for writing or the current writing is decelerated in its creativity. The reality of it is that this condition is conditional.

All of life's a perpetual prediction predicated on perception. It's based on what we're feeling. The movie production we're starring in while the reel-to-reel keeps reeling. The hand the dealer's dealing. Writers block's blocking me because I'm stifled by my feelings.

Words make this hurt so real the inscriptions hurt me still. Life stole something definitive from me and the thief continues to steal. Identity theft in truth and the writings on the wall. I want to write until my death, but the tears start to fall. There's a story in every teardrop, wish I could write em all.

There's a battle in every heartache, wish I could fight em all. I keep em bottled up tight. Clutch my pillow staring into dark places I wish I could forget at night. Vacillate between the things I know not to do and the things I might. Stare at the

49

The Artist

*blank pages, eyes filled with tears, too
afraid to write. A writer blocked by
writers' block*

****Boost: That unction of artistic
function on the inside of you must come
forth! The greatest tragedy in life is
dying with the seed of potential still on
the inside. ****

Let Me Go

*Reading and reading, over and over
thinking of the things I hold on to. I've
held on to a painful past with memories of
me and the "you" I belong to. I've held
on to things I shouldn't have done and
things I should gon' do. I've held on to
many lies and some things I've always
known true.*

*In all my clutching and holding, my
forever is a fleeting moment. Now in this
exact enactment, there's a necessity that
we own it. The blind blindly guide,
blindfolded deception and darkness is all
I can see. I'm puzzled, the harmful things
I continue to hold onto just will not let go
of me.*

The Artist
Two, Broken

*She heard the insults growing up. She
heard all the name calling. She can't see
things for what they really are, the tears
just won't stop falling. Determined to
move on and love again, her heart just
keeps stalling then she falls in love with
me. The most dangerous place for a
person with low self-esteem to be.
Mismatched broken pieces driven and
tossed on life's sea. A man too selfish to
love her, too broken to let her leave.
We're two broken people too broken to let
it be.*

The Artist
In a Room Full of People

*Here in a room full of people, but I'm here all alone. I
hear laughing, joking and talking. Can smell the smoke
from someone smoking but there's nobody here but me;
here in a full room filled with people. Conversations are
meaningless, swollen with folly and pretend yet there's
talk without end. Disagreement and contention because
there's talk without friends. Here in a room full of
people, but there's nobody here. I'm alone. They see me
standing on the wall, the strongman appears tall, but
they don't see my fears. The crying's camouflaged so
they can't see my tears. See I been screaming since birth.
Unsure of my worth, continually curse the earth
wondering why my momma had me just to wind up here?
Direction so unclear, here in a room full of people. In
the hustle and bustle of our world and its' ways, it's a
struggle and tussle to exist with each day.*

The Artist

The words stir inside but I don't know what to say so I exist in clamor, drowning in noise here in a room full of people. Turn the music up please!

Brokenness can't describe it. Struggling to heal from what hurts me while I attempt to provide emotional support for my children and wife. The whole time no one knows how I fight for my life. Easy to hide in the crowd. Long as I'm quiet nobody notices, don't talk too loudly. It's not manly to be confused, life's out of control. Keep running for my life but there's nowhere to go. Hold to God's hand, feels I want to let go in this big empty room filled with people I don't know. I'm here alone.

I'm in a room full of people and I feel myself dying, withering with pride, mold forming inside and the stench or the moisture from old stagnant evil has the onlookers looking but there's nothing to see! Let's go, keep it moving, nothing to see here, unless you're entertained by pain, hopelessness and fear. Heart beats and then stops like I die over and over, the skin grows clammy, sweat drops in thick drops. Drip, drop, drip, drop, drip.... I'm right here in this place irrelevant as can be with plenty to say but no one to hear me, in a room full of people.

I want to cry, wanna scream, wanna run full speed but there's not enough space. I'm boxed in from within and arrested by rage. Infuriated emotionally, standing on stage expected to be strong, perform and achieve all the things that are possible, but I just don't believe. Wanna laugh, wanna cry, wanna fall flat and die rather than live in this misery, in a world that's still missing me. I never existed, I lived but you missed it. Wait, was I even

The Artist

alive? Reading the story of my life and in this part, I die.
In this part of the story, I strangle the lie. The last
chapter and there's silence, no words and no laughter.
Death creeps up on my character faster and faster. It
doesn't matter to me. I'm sick of the violence. I'm sick of
the noise. I'm sick of the men around me living like boys.
Sick of the women complaining about the failures of
men. Once I'm sick of being sick, I get sick all again
because they're all still talking...and me, I'm in a room
full of people.

The Artist
Lost My Mind Losing You

Losing my mind slowly. Staring in the mirror at a man acting like he don't know me, but I know him. I know his smile left when she was gone. I know he's always felt loneliness, but now he feels alone. Caught up on the inside of insidious aesthetics. Hypocritical poetics still word after word after word. Brutal calamities plague me; your voice is all I heard.

I wonder what you ate today. I wonder if I run into you will I even know what to say. You have my heart. You are my soul. I'm forced to wake up every day hopeless, waiting to grow old. I'm losing my mind slowly. Been in love before or at least I thought I was until I met someone who loved me. Until I knew all that love could be. I found forever in your eyes and the more and more I try to hold back tears, the more and more I cry. They can't be wiped away....to live a life apart from you causes a weeping that's there to stay.

Your name's etched in the layers of my loins. My tomorrow may never come. Next week I may never see. Broken hearted without you so next week doesn't matter to me. Always trying to do what's best and to make the right decisions but this time it caused me pain; may never breathe again. I may never find a friend because I'm sure I'll never look. I'll always love you deeply so here's the always that it took. It makes no sense to let go of a love I'll never find. Write senselessly from this empty place while I feel myself losing my mind.

The Artist

Constitutional

Surrounded by mechanisms of biological chaos. Predetermined transitions by divinity, it's impossible to stay lost. Charged by Misdirection, it's impossible to pay cost. The fruit of the moment is imminent. The wages of consumption are imminent. Feeling full. Tired of bull. Tired of having feelings for people that just ain't feeling me. Tired of living life for those I'd die for, realizing that's what killing me. Striving to see millions but they can't see what I can see. We close our eyes to what's real. Tell lies about how we feel. Write it in words and immortalize it so after death, you read it still.

Words exist outside of reality. Fictitious writing scribbled about real life everyday fallacy. Someone please call 911. The black family's being assassinated and the bloodline's holding the gun. The ancestors watching the news shaking their head at this confusion. The next generation is so wise, their wisdom created this new illusion. What would Jesus do? What would Trayvon do? Maybe buy M&M's instead of skittles.... some say he should've been home, but the constitution says different. I fight a fight I know I'll win so that's why I continue fighting. I jot it down as we go along so you'll wonder 'Is he serious, or just writing?'

HIS FAMILY

His Family

Her Healing

Be my guest of honor;
this invitation's to my insanity.
RSVP as soon as possible,
touch base with the man in me.

Bandage and balm these emotions;
fit the broken pieces.
Resuscitate the dead place;
apply pressure to this bleeding

No it's not your place to heal me;
not your responsibility to do.
I don't want to be burdensome,
but I give you permission too.

There's a power you have,
I've recognized it always.
Recognized that we are still in place,
because of times we all prayed.

See more than a woman in you,
you make me more of a man.
It's not that you're obligated to help me;
but please, I know you can.

His Family

Soul Findings

No one knows but her.
We found each other
in the loneliest lingering,
no one knew where we were.

I cried decades of sorrow, she
caught and kissed my tears.
Felt abandoned and lost,
her bosom nestled the fears.

Didn't understand her strength.
She loved me past perception.
Eyes sifted through me
with surgery like precision,
she saw God's reflection

She's life's definition, the
heartbeat of true purpose.
Me, I discover her more and more,
treasuring her timeless worth

We are eternally sun and moon,
each world, we hold together.
We found each other in loneliness,
our destiny is forever

His Family

A Father

Lying next to my wife, children all tucked in, barely living life, filled with discontent and strife. A million unanswered questions race through my head. Wonder why you didn't want me, was I unworthy of love? Did I not deserve attention; your affection and hugs? I'm not here to whine and I'm not here to cry, I just stumbled through life without you and keep asking myself why?

If I had a father, I would call you right now. I'd ask you how to love this woman? I just don't know how. Ask you about sex, fighting, about sports; but you were never around, nowhere to be found.

I wish I had a father, sit on the bank together fishing. We fry it up when we're done, watch you love on my sons. I wish I had a father, help me sort through broken pieces and make sense of all this madness, yet this father I never had. The man responsible for making me didn't even care or bother, now I'm blessed with my own children still here wishing I had a father.

I'm somewhat disgruntled, at times I'm just mad, thinking about cub scout meetings and my friends had their dad and they always got mad cause their pops felt compelled to reach out to your son because you weren't there. The badges I earned and the knots that I tied, the fights I would lose and the tears that I cried when I lay down at night and wondered where you were, what you looked like or what was I here for? Would I recognize you? Do I call you dad? Probably not cause you're the best father I never had.

His Family

*No need bellyaching over milk that's been spilt, the
bridge that's been burnt cause I'm laying here still with
a childhood that's filled with the scars and the pain and
I'm laying here playing this old sad song again. The
thoughts they won't cease, they're in my head buzzing
while my kids need their dad and my wife needs her
husband. Paralyzed. Crippled. A shell of the man I could
be.... because I never had a father be a father to me*

His Family

Daddy's Biggest Fears

No place to hide for a man without a guide. A man lost without direction, forced to face his recollections of cheating at the hand he was dealt. Stares into the eyes of his wrongdoings and holds hands with guilt. A man lost and uncertain, flirts with worthlessness in worth. Disgusted by his hurt. Misunderstood by many. He left so many broken hearts; he himself felt plenty. If there is anything that anyone would believe as true, it's the fact that you've never felt pain until your daughter is hurt by a man like you.

Artwork by Johnathan "Cool B" Brand

His Family

The Greatest

*Don't remember much about momma, she never had
much to say. She wasn't around when I was young,
that's the part I'll always hate. I wanted her at PTA, or
talent shows when the kids would laugh. Other kids had
their mom and dad, I thought mine was mad. Perhaps I
had done something wrong and caused them not to care.
I just remember growing up as a child without having a
parent anywhere.*

*Never heard much about my Dad, he was only a guess in
my head. I made up stories to tell the teachers,
sometimes I said they were dead. Sometimes I gave them
good jobs overseas to reinforce their excuse. Now that
I'm older I know why they never came; they didn't want
to. Mom did send me a pair of skates, royal blue with a
stripe on the side. I wanted to keep them on day and
night because they were from mom, I wore 'em with
pride.*

*Nevertheless, I had the greatest grandmother a child
could ever need. We grew so close; I was there for her
and she was there for me. We ate fried bologna
sandwiches almost every day, scrambled eggs or grilled
cheese. I would give her insulin shots in the stomach, she
fanned me while I was asleep. It was one of those paper
fans from the church with the full color family picture on
the front.*

*I knew there were so many nights for us when she just
wasn't feeling well. She wouldn't complain, just keep*

His Family

*fanning me, I knew her well enough to tell. She lay there
after she thought I was sleeping. I could hear her moan
and grunt because she was feeling pain in her body. I felt
so helpless. Paralyzed and incapable of comforting her
suffering. She never stopped fanning me but for what it's
worth if there was something I could do, then I would've
taken her pain away and did the best I knew. I still feel
hurt from my absent parents and the things I felt I
missed, but I smile and thank God I had a grandmother
that I could write about like this.*

In Loving Memory Esther Mae Miller – Thank You

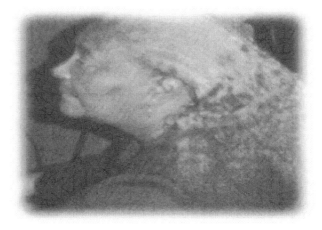

Perhaps it seems I'm getting a little mushy; I may as well
tell you why, right? Well, whenever we revisit painful
places, we reopen wounds that needed healing.
Dislocated, emotional breakings of the soul that went
unattended, leading to a healed dislocated position.
Every time the person makes an emotional flinch in that
direction, it causes them pain. Ouch. I could write
countless works of art expressing the deep lustful

His Family

cravings of my sexual appetite, but I know you want more than that. How can we be in a meaningful trusting author/reader relationship except I give you the best of me? The only way I can give you the best of me is to give you the rest of me so here it is. C. Miller.

Most men never come to a place of vulnerability in life long enough to admit how badly they're hurting. Living day in and day out with the weight of every traumatic experience ever suffered. Have you ever felt the painful memories of a tormenting childhood? A broken relationship that didn't turn out like you expected. A person you loved and trusted that not only disappointed you, but never bothered explain why they made the decisions they made? Yea, me too. The weird part of it all is that after I've grown older, have my own wife and children, done quite well for myself, but the memory of it haunts me to the point it looms in the content of most of my writing. An adult male suffering emotional suffocation.

I remember my grandmother had these weird French windows in the front room of the house. The windows had a crazy crank handle configuration that you had to turn so the doors coverings of the window would open. We had the plaid couch that I believe every family had at some point. She kept the couch positioned right under the window and that's where I first felt pain. In the evenings after school, I would jump my hopeful naïve youthfulness up on the couch, situated on my knees with my elbows propped in the dusty, dead roach covered lattice so I could gaze out the window. Many days, so

His Family

many evenings when I could've been playing, I was waiting for my mom or dad to pull up in the yard. Concocting deep thoughts and playful imaginations about how I wanted my life to be. I live in that window, playing make-believe. Waiting on one of them to want to be where I was or have me wherever they were. It never happened. I don't know when I stopped staring out the window, but I know this, I never stopped hoping they would pull up. This is one of the places that writing filled in the void. I could empty my cup of discontented delusion into the oceans of possibility. Even though I stopped jumping up on that plaid couch, I kept writing about parents in my poems. Poetry has been good to me form as far back as I can remember.

My 12th grade literature teacher gave me the best gift possible of my entire life when we had to read Hamlet as course assignment. The character Polonius said something to his son that has lived in me from the day I read it until now, "This above all; to thine own self, be true." I always absorbed that and understood it to mean, when the time comes, you're face to face with expressing what you feel or making decisions, do what's best for you. Be true to yourself. Say what's true. I wrote the next few poems in this book about my parents.

My mother and I were apart most of my young life. For a child with unanswered questions, it made it hard to understand. Most of the way I interpreted it was that she didn't love me, she didn't care. The interpretation of that relationship will show up and reflect how that felt as a child. My 2nd grade teacher, Mrs. Willamina Shird,

His Family

taught my mom, my cousins and lived long enough to teach me. She spoke real highly of my mom. I was always super proud to hear things about her; everyone boasts of how smart she was and the similarities we have in appearance and character. People see her picture and tell me I look just like her. Felt good and all, but nothing would've felt better than seeing her pull up in that gravel driveway and say "son, momma came to get you". I'm much older now and I understand, I just missed her, that's all.

My dad was in Natchez for most of his life from what I understand. I met him a couple of times. Before he died the past October, I had taken my boys to meet him, they would have a visual. He seemed like a cool guy for the most part, he just didn't bother being dad to me. I'm not sure what I felt, whether it was embarrassment or what because when I joined the Army, I would write him letters thinking he would be proud of my decision to serve in the military. He never wrote back. In excitement, I was telling my mom the entire time that I was writing him. She never said, but it seemed important to her that I endear him as dad and do my best to connect. I didn't have the heart to tell her he didn't want to be bothered. I made up stories and told her lies like he and I were making a connection. Led her to believe we had this awesome relationship in the makings. One of the lies was so major, it backfired on me! I told my mom that my dad wanted to take me to a fight in Las Vegas. Go figure! Guess which one? The Tyson vs. Hollifield fight! I called her like we were there and made up this

His Family

elaborate description of the hotels and laced it full of
fancy exaggerations about the crowded, big-city
activities going on around us. Everything was a go,
until...yep, you guessed it, controversial rapper Tupac
Shakur shot that night. The nationally televised news
report covering the Hollifield fight explained that there
was a big fight in the lobby of the casino where the event
happened, which happened to be the location my dad and
I were residing. Couple hours later, same rapper died.
Now this had my then unsuspecting momma at home
worried about her lying ass son in this city with his slow-
moving daddy while all this commotion transpires. She
just played along with it all. Never even said much else
about the fight or my dad. Times like those helped me
realize how much I missed them both. The same lies I
told the teachers about my parents working overseas and
having these awesome jobs as spies and translators,
continued even into manhood. Not lying to impress
nobody, just wanted to put a figure of a parent in place.

I'm so thankful that they were in my life the time I was
blessed to have them though. No need crying over
spilled milk but who's crying? This is writing. True story
and like I told you before, writing is my therapy. Let me
share a couple of them with you.

His Family

Dear Dad,

You're gone now, there's nothing left to say. I'll never hear your voice again, it's horrible feeling this way. Funny thing is the way I prayed for you when I was a kid. Grown up realizing if I'm not careful, my kids could feel just like I did. Only difference is I recognized it and still have time to fix it. But you, you're dead, gone for good and my while life well, you missed it. Now you'll never get this note from the son you never had, and me, I'll never mail it to the man that was never dad.

Love you

I adopted a cold-hearted, callous "Tupac" approach to my feelings about my dad, or the absence thereof. To my surprise, all my feelings were pretentious preambles to a long life of made-up emotions for the purpose of masking the hurtful consequence of what I never wanted to face. When my father died, I cried just as hard. Not only had I never known him, but I never would. Not only had I never loved him, I never could.

His Family

Birthday Cakes

Mom has gotten older and her health is not the best.
Never built a good relationship with her, hers and mine
is not the best. This test my malnourished manhood, feels
like I'm even less than significantly myself. Mom had me
then she left.

People say I'm too old to think about it, I make myself
believe I don't. I pray it doesn't come up again, it always
does when I don't want. Feels like she resented me. Like
my birth was inconvenient. Like I'm the residue of my
lying dad that told her "I love you" and didn't mean it.

She loves me with self-centered expectations, who she
imagines me to be. I understand because we haven't
known each other; I played mommy make-believe. She's
been my real-life fairy-tale, I just never wrote the ending.
Made up all those letters I sat and read she never
bothered sending. If we could spend more time together,
surely, I'd be spending because she was my best
imaginary friend, I ever bothered befriending.

Made up the candles blown out on my birthday cakes,
the ones I never had. Had my first party at 41, it almost
made me sad. PTA meetings, I lied to teachers about
having a mom and dad. My daughter will probably grow
up herself and write this poem to her dad. It's life.

I had to make up my parents, felt like what I was
supposed to do. I had no him, I had no you, too
embarrassed to tell the truth. An emotionally disabled

His Family

*dude, others mocked the man in me. Much like childhood
and living alone, nothing can stop the man in me!*

*Won't tell her, I'm writing it cause like I said, she's
older, it's over and I care. I just write because this is
what I felt, longing for a mother that wasn't there.*

His Family

Insomnia

Sitting on the couch broken half in two, one piece is James Smith, the other half is you. What am I? Everyone that cares, I push them away without even bothering to try. Drowning and dying in gallons of tears when I'm not even crying. You are my earth, wind and fire. You have always been the only acceptance I've long for, you are my desire. I missed you mom.

I needed a momma. I needed a dad that came to boy scout meetings and wouldn't fail me. I needed to know you, what happened back then, all I wanted was for you to tell me. Tell me about him. Tell me I had brothers and what happened back when. What happened back then and why did everybody leave me? I needed you. Needed you to affirm me, now because of it all, I'm here on the couch sad with nobody to call. Nobody at all. I treat women badly, misuse them repeatedly. I'm hungry for affection and these women keep feeding me. I'm hungry for acceptance, hungry for affirmation. Pouring it out in words to appease my frustration.

Nobody to let know I'm here dying inside. My wife does all she can, but I'm dying inside. You never held my hand; I can't remember a hug. Can't remember your voice, can't remember your love. All I hear are noises and unrelenting voices. Can't dwell on the past because everybody's got choices. I came out of you. I know it came as a surprise, but I still have your eyes. Some say I have your lips. Our family says I have your smarts, but I just wish I had your heart because that was the missing part. Inside I'm cold and heartless.

Wish I had gotten time and love from you or maybe Dad. Wish I knew how to wish for things I wanted but sadly never had.

His Family

*Wish I could tell the boys all these great things about you.
Don't say a word, on their own they're even starting to doubt
you. No grandparents call on their birthdays, they're coping
with life without you. They're learning more and more how to
doubt you. Me? I've been this way since I was two. Wasn't no
you there for me then and now still, no you. A lot of ways I
break the finger off my point of view. Who cares what I have
to say? Who cares how I might feel? I live and keep it bottled
up, because I just can't keep it real.*

His Family

Wow!!!! That glance into the times of those writings took me through a little bit of an emotional spin. My mom and I have come so far over the past few years. Her willingness and presence impacted my life exponentially, reinforcing my self-esteem and assured my sense of confidence. It's funny how we grow into adults only to learn that all our behavior up until that point has been formed and fashioned by the ways we were treated as children, helping better understanding how the pieces fit. The things we remember, challenges and the places we grew up contributed to our overall perception of what life is, how we're supposed to face it. After all these years, I can look back and see how everything that was happening, was preparing me to sit here on this couch right now and write these words.

Jackson Mississippi, 4104 Warner Avenue, the incubator of my life protecting, nurturing and teaching me. Nursed and cared for by the most unbelievable grandmother imaginable! I love you Esther Mae! As a matter of fact, there were people in the neighborhood that knew it was only her and I that lived there. The organ player helped get us to church and continued to come by, picking me up after my grandmother had gotten older and the pain of aging started taking its toll. I.V. Berry was declared my godfather and he was a barber, my godmother, "Momma Rose" was a beautician. Not sure how they decided who would do what and when, but they took turns grooming me. I guess if he had time, he'd cut my hair, if she had time, she'd put a curl in it. That's right curl! Cream of Nature,

His Family

World of Curls, Stay FRO spray activator, drip slanging curl. Mess your couch up with a grease stain, curl! They did that. My Aunt Gladys made sure we made it to doctor appointments and my big cousin Bird did all the running around to guarantee I had whatever I needed for school. Bird had three children and she would try to include me whenever she would do things with her kids. That's how I learned to ride a bicycle and skate, because of her. Her knee baby, Anneshia Renee would be in the window fussing because I was learning to ride a bike on her bicycle. "Momma! Get that big ole boy off my bike! That big ole fat boy! He gon break it!" "Shut up gurl! That boy ain't gon hurt that damn bike! If he do, hell I bought it!" Neshia and I shared the same birthday. She died of cancer July 4th, 2017 at far too young of an age. Left three beautiful daughters that I really wish understood the fun of growing up in the days when danger wasn't as imminent. Even with her fussing, I loved that ole girl! RIP Anneshia Renee.

Back then, I didn't really pay much attention to name brands because all we got were our food stamps and my grandmas social security check once a month went straight to the necessities! Bird was a little younger, in fact she was about two years younger than my mom. I wouldn't tell her kids at school were picking on me because I was wearing hand-me-down clothes from my godmother's 24-year-old son, but she figured it out. Can you imagine what it was like going to school with these silk button down shirts on with the big collars on them in the 3rd grade? I was the punchline to the jokes every day,

His Family

until she started trying to buy me different things, so my entire outfit was not a laughingstock. It was cool. There were even people in the neighborhood or at the church who would bring food by when they got their food stamps. They'd drop those blocks of government cheese off and if 2 or 3 people gave us cheese, we could put a couple blocks in the freezer. Before long we had a nice little cheese stash. I smile when I hear other people talking about that same cheese and the way they remember it. Most people refer to using it for making "the best grilled cheese". Me? That's not quite how I remember it. Matter fact, I don't remember it like that at all. Put it in the cast iron skillet, brown that bread until it's crunchy black, cheese still ain't melted! It's 40 years later and I haven't made that cheese melt yet! Whatever though, because it fed me and served its purpose. Plenty burnt bread cheese sandwiches. You know why I told you all that? Me neither. Guess I just enjoy talking to you! You're alright with me. Now, so far, I've kept you filled in on why certain writings were in place. I probably won't do that very much for the rest of this book because I must save some of the stuff for another publishing work or my family will starve. I have a wife and three children. My daughter I had from a previous relationship and she's my only girl. Absolutely gorgeous! Then I have two strong handsome young men by my super supportive wife of 21 years. I haven't been the easiest guy in the world to live with and I will give you a little bit of all those relationships in the next few writings. All of it's not pretty. All of it's not the amazing

His Family

love story that everyone likes to read in books but all of it's real. It's real and it's really me so what can I say?

Thin Walls

Getting harder to love them both, it's like I have to
choose sides. My dad always seems mad with mom, at
night I hear her cry. They're pretending when we're at
dinner, the tension they can't hide. I'm lonely, losing my
appetite, playing in my food and crying inside. Cover my
head with my pillow, trying to go to sleep at night. Harsh
echoes in the hallway, they trying to whisper while
they're fighting.

Unusual headaches every day for me, sleepless nights at
night. No mom to read me bedtime stories. No dad to
teach me right. Empty trance-like state of mind, to my
parents, I don't exist. I feel my dad may hurt my mom
and I'm the reason for all this.

Locked up playing video games, screaming for help, but
no one hears it. Angry faint whispers of arguing, it's
stopped but I still hear it. Bullied by stress and neglect,
lonely abandon I hold dear. Zombie-like motions
limping thru life, shackled with this fear. Lego blocks
my therapy, the only toys I can't destroy. Parents spent
all my childhood fighting. Ignored their only boy.

Ignored their own creation, I still hurt down inside.
Unusual way of driving people away; that's normal
behavior, right? Blocking memories from back then,
don't want to see what used to be. Dysfunction in a
forgotten memory that still remembers me.

His Family

At First

This unexpected event's troubling me. You died from this life not living a day in mine, I feel like my life's smothering me. Emotions mixed and guarded. Mad at you for making me the son you never bothered to father. You never bothered to bother. In your death you've died and left me again, it's hitting me even harder. Even more now daddy, I have to hear people apologize. "I'm sorry for your loss", that's sweet but for me, long ago you died.

At first, I wanted you round. At first, I wanted to know you. At first, I thought about important things in my life I wanted to show you. At first, I would be excited to hear about you at all. The excitement died while waiting by a phone, you never called. At first, I wanted my kids to have a grandpa to look up to. At first, I wanted to have just one promise that you stuck to. At first, I wanted you to hear all about this awesome woman I wanted to marry. Now she's beside me helping me look for my name that's not on your obituary. At first, I felt guilty you died because I didn't think I would feel as bad. That was before I remembered you died and left me never being my dad.

His Family

How's it going so far? I hope you're enjoying the things you're experiencing because I'm loving the time we're having. Would be a complete disgrace if I didn't share a piece I wrote for a special lady. I've invested time learning the unequivocal wisdom of the female mind. There's nothing more magical than the function and expression of a feminine personality. Our relationship as writer/reader is too premature for me to share with you the nature of my female interaction but let's just say I've spent time learning how incredibly complex the woman is. I love it. I love their power! I love their influence and I absolutely love the hidden sensuality that every woman possesses! I say that because I have one of the most amazing sisters you ever want to meet. Divinely unique and probably doesn't even feel she's as wonderful as she is. She stood by me, believed in me, defended me, forgave me, all without being judgmental, continually loving me through it all. I want to share something I wrote for her once and I only ask that you keep her in your prayers. I love you sis!! Dedicated to Keekee & Tyrese

*****Boost: Not only do we have but one life to live, you only have one of each particular loved one to love. Make your relationship with them matter. Let everybody in your life know they matter. Every chance you get, every time you have a moment, by any means necessary! Always let them know*****

His Family

Sister

I been thinking about you all morning!!! I typed the words "good morning" but something gripped me in the mind.

Before I finished typing the message, ready to press send too fast, I wondered what my message would say if this day was my last. If I didn't have my sister, my loved one and my friend.... what would I type in the message box this morning before I press send?

I thought about our conversations, each one tried to remember. The serious ones in October, the funny ones in December. The one about our families in the middle of July. The time you told me I forgot your birthday, that one made me cry. The ones I cannot recall we had no matter how hard I try. Still sitting here wondering what I would text if today was my day to die.

I'd tell her "behind every dark cloud there's a silver line", and that I do believe. Behind every silver lining there's another dark cloud, keep living and you'll see. I'd tell her she deserves to be loved, settle for nothing less. I'd tell her I wish I was a better brother because she deserves the best. I'd tell her life will challenge her, she may want to give in. Remind her this world's not hers to change, just here for her to live in.

See life's filled with inconsistency and goes by way too fast. I never want to take for granted a "right now" moment that I know in a moment will pass. In all the wishes I have ever wished; I wish I made more moments

His Family

last. Then the day I'm dying what could I text to a sister that's like no other? Me? I probably wouldn't text at all.... I'd call and tell her I love her. I love you sis

His Family

Keep your eyes on the prize! I've heard this phrase enough for three lifetimes. Never quite understood the full value of this truth until I had taken my eyes off the prize. You don't miss your water until your well runs dry? No, you don't miss your water until you're thirsty and you're used to having water to drink. You're used to having someone to love and know that they love you back. We've been married for over 21 years and when I tell you there are so many distractions that can draw you away from the nurturing focus necessary to maintain a healthy matrimonial union, believe me. To be honest, my wife and I were just kids, both of us were running from relationships back home that we didn't have the love or maturity to be involved in. Go figure right. The best way to get out of one situation is to immerse yourself in another! Or at least that's a popular thinking. Not understanding life, love or the importance of trust and respect, we caused each other a lot of pain and heartache. I don't know if either one of us felt that it would last this long and I'm pretty sure there were times our behaviors were deliberate sabotage, subconsciously intending the demise of the union, but we're still here. It's been hard. It's been hurtful. It's been painful, excruciatingly painful at times, but we're still here.

So, how did we do it? Let me make it clear, we aren't there yet because each day is filled with choices and at any given time, anybody can make a choice that may lead to the detriment of their committed vows. Best thing I can say, keep your eyes on the prize. I don't know if anyone fully understands the indispensable

His Family

depths of committed love involved in making it to "The Rocking Chairs"! My wife picked up on it much sooner than me and she has been the frontline soldier in our relationship every step of the way! I've never had anyone show commitment, dedication and affection to anybody the way she has for our children and me.

One time, Puff, my very best friend in the whole world referred to life with your spouse as stated above, "The Rocking Chairs". He equated the grand finale, the end of the race, the 50- and 60-year anniversary celebrations to "The Rocking Chairs". Picture the wooden chairs on the porch, the small coffee table between them for drinking coffee and looking out across the yard. The couple talks about the arguments, break ups and experiences they faced which all seem nothing now. The fun places you've visited and the friends you made. The ups and downs have meaning, but neither of them understand what they mean until they've made it to the chairs. Watching the kids and grandkids pull up in the yard with their young families, looking forward sharing the joys of newborns, graduations, weddings, and family vacations with that person. In sickness and in health! Making it! The Golden years! The Gold Metal to this long marathon race of commitment that we call marriage. He explained the necessity of having that as a goal and how important it is in the decision to press forward at every stage! Press forward and go higher!!! Without the perspective that keeps the end in sight, you'll never make it. Except you aim at a target, you can never hit it.

His Family

So, this beautifully committed woman that said "I do" to my black ass over 22 years ago, explains through all her behavior that she's determined to make it to the chairs. I learn every day that there are better ways to love her and I'm humbled by the reality that God gave her to me, and I don't deserve her at all. This is where it gets complicated because as I type, while you and I are in the middle of this poetic exhibit, the promise I made to give you the most transparently genuine version of myself possible is becoming the sword of conviction. I haven't been an honest man. I haven't been a good father. I haven't been a faithful husband and at 45 years old, I'm still wondering what I want to be when I grow up. Regretfully, I choose to let you see the ugliest part of me. See, the craziest thing a man can experience is a life full of rambling and uncertainty. The worst feeling a man can give to a woman, is making her wrestle with the uncertainty of not being enough, not being loved, not knowing if you're with her, or just going along for comfort! She has someone beside her, but she's lying in bed alone. Let me reiterate before we go any further, in no way is this intended to be advice or a claim to the way things should be in a marriage. Once either has done wrong that causes emotional damage to the other, it's completely up to that person to decide if they want to continue in the relationship. What I will say without reservation is this, 1) whatever you decide to do as a couple is nobody's business but the two of you. Nobody has a vote, say or contribution and nobody judges whatever decision you choose. 2) Please, listen carefully, if you have someone you love, and you know they love

His Family

you, do not hurt them. Do not betray them or misuse their trust.

That's the only advice I feel is worth giving at this point in my life. Whatever you discover in the words of this poetry, can be taken and used at your own discretion, but it's mainly me just sharing my life, love and encounters. The two advice points I just gave, that's all I got. Seems most men suffer through many similar experiences. Since the beginning we've fallen and succumb to some of the same manipulative tricks, the same seductions and doesn't seem it's getting better. Eventually, I feel it will harden the heart of our women to the point they have no faith in us what-so-ever except we change. Adjust our personal behavior and assume the responsibility of all the hurt we've caused our wives and children over the years. This is my resolve anyways. Pray for me in this endeavor and hope you enjoy the next few poems.

His Family

Good Question

Children calling for daddy. Wife calling her "husband".
Husband calling on God and struggling with some
questions.

How do I lead this family?
How do I teach them right?
Why do I toss and turn when everybody's sleep at night?
Why do I feel anxiety when everything seems right? Why
can't we agree, eliminate some of the fighting?

Why won't she ever listen?
Why don't my own kids mind?
Why is there no logic for the illogical in my mind?
Why do I even bother?
Why am I still here trying?
Why am I counterfeiting a smile when inside, I'm hurt
and crying?
Why am I asking why? There's nobody replying.
Why ask Iyanla to fix my life, looking forward to dying.

Now wife's fast asleep, children playing their games. Me,
I'm on my knees, tears falling while I'm praying. Heart
racing fast, wrestling with the Maker. Hoping He'll have
mercy, let me love her before He take her. Hoping He
shows favor and showers us with His blessings. But if
not, Your will be done; least answer my questions!

His Family

Live Through It

It's likened to a newborn baby. My
way of communicating's not
communicating lately; maybe I'm
speaking "baby". "Goo Goo-
GahGah" Contractions and labor
pains relating. I know you're there
but it's so unfair because I'm the
man and you're the lady. Complete
miscarriage of our happy marriage.

Impregnated you with hopeful ideas
I had for us and "we". You were
expectantly hoping for superman
when Clark Kent's all I can be. My
visions probably robbing us, short-
sighted all I see, bifocals may be
what I need? Our children have
been our everything.

Our first born was our commitment,
now he's gone and seems we're
dying. Feel so far away from you;
I'm lost, broken and crying. Men
don't cry, so I hide the tears,
making me broken and lying.
Losing hope of making it through
this as "us" cause you and I are
hopelessly dying.

His Family

I just write the words I never say;
emasculated, scribbling words that
fade away. They perish and
dwindle. They vanish and
disappear. A marriage hauled away
pronounced still born, suffocated by
pillows of fear.

His Family

Biggest Fight

*We just had the biggest fight; I broke furniture and all.
She sipped Moscato, threw the bottle at me, it crashed
against the wall. She screamed and yelled in anger, I
was every name she could call. I'm typing this wondering
in my mind, is there any 'making up' at all because we
just had the biggest fight!*

*We just had the biggest fight; seems it was worse this
time. Thoughts of saying things to her I never imagined
ran through my mind. I slammed the door, cut my phone
off, she can't reach me if she trying. Having the phone off
hurts me more, can't get her off my mind and we just had
the biggest fight.*

*We just had the biggest fight. It's like there's no going
back. I keep hearing her scream "it's over", trying more
would be an act. Once love is lost and trust is broken it's
hard to get it back. It's hard for me to focus at work, the
words keep playing back.*

*We just had the biggest fight. Don't know if there's much
left. Asking why bother doing bad together when I can do
bad all by myself? Asking is it worth the pain; feeling the
worst I've ever felt? The more I give myself to her, the
more I lose myself and we just had the biggest fight!*

*We just had the biggest fight! Pretty sure we're breaking
up. No staying together after this, no way we're making
up. No way to overlook what's happening, whole world is
shaken up. This violently volatile place we're in, not a
good place for us, not after what we just had.*

His Family

At work distracted, going through motions, can hardly
concentrate. Thinking of calling to talk about it, not sure
what I could say. Not sure if there's a way she and I
could communicate. Not sure if it's even worth it, hell
what difference would it make? How much can one heart
take? How many times do I bend over backwards loving
her before I break? Every time we're together seems it
leaves me feeling down. She probably feels the same as
me, we're not speaking now. Can't imagine us even being
apart, it's hurts me by just writing. Confused, not
knowing what to do, but I'm damn sure sick of fighting.
We just had the biggest fight

His Family

Matrimony

Is there a possibility of time travel? Can we return to points in life where we talked and depart from Babel? Is selfishness the way we end, our friendship's held for ransom? Have we strategically joined the ranks of the failed relationship chances? Chances are we're taking chances on things and never gambled on us. Single-handedly I gambled on schemes and never gambled on trust. Never gambled on love, gambling was never my thing. I never gambled on you and me, chose to gamble on flings.

I'm crying inside and calling for you, but of course you probably don't hear it. The demons are tearing my soul apart and I'm too proud to let you near it. I see you dying in the distance and I should be there to save your life. My matrimonial vows need resuscitating and I should give CPR to our life. Life support to my wife, be even better to my kids. I regret the things I've done, can't seem to live with all the things I did.

I fought many battles and won wishing many didn't have to die, now in the battle of my life and seems no matter how hard I try, death is imperative. We are dying. A brilliant narrative. By the time anyone sees the need for you and me, we will have lost it all. We'll be people of much substance that lived lives with no substance at all. Substance abuse asking what's the use? Choosing to be users. Two lovers with the potential to love in love with being losers. We lost. Goodbye love

His Family

The Vows

We've been looking into "new beginnings". "Happily-ever-after" never lasted, I've been thinking about redoing endings. Vowed a vow until death do us part. Death's ugly mar tore both our hearts and left this ugly scar. We were the best at the "rich or poorer", seeing the rich with riches left our poor ass wanting more. Don't even know what we were striving for? Wish we could click our heels together, be back in Bell county court.

Wish we could have a piece of peace of mind. Wish that Justice of the Peace had contraptions to rewind the hands of time. Day to day depression, feels like we're wasting time. Keep hoping I could win your trust, other times, feels like I'm lying. We fought hard, there's no denying. Been together since forever, I know it's worth us trying.

Guess it's part of this crazy life. Crazy family, crazy strife, I now pronounce you, crazy wife! Crazy wife and I'm your crazy husband. We take the bitter with the sweet, a crazy you for a crazy me. You know what still amazes me? The fact that I'm out of words. Nothing said, nothing heard. Silence. No explanations. No reasoning left for us and no, we don't know the outcome. Win some we lose some. Way it's always been, and it probably always will.... until death do us part, even now I love you still. Think I'm crazy?

His Family

The Wife's Wants

Longing for you to hold me, but you never had the time.
Needed a shoulder to lean on, you never heard me
crying. Called out when I felt empty, but the TV was too
loud. At times I wanted to be alone with you, but you
were mixed in with the crowd.

You brought me gifts and flowers, that was nice to do.
You took me on expensive trips, but I just wanted you.
Long hours at work to make more money is all you ever
knew. I know you wanted to give me the world, but I just
wanted you

I just wanted your attention. I just wanted your hand. I
just wanted your protection, you to be there as my man.
Just wanted to be close to you, love you hard as I can.
Now I just want to run away from this broken feeling I
can't stand.

I lay besides you at night and I can feel us far apart.
Tossing and turning restlessly because I don't feel you in
my heart. I knew you had gotten the best of me; I knew
when this feeling started. Knew that my deep love for you
would leave me hurt and brokenhearted

I'm dying slowly and deteriorating with this lifeless hope
inside me. Living life alone loving you while you lay
right here beside me. Wish I had died, but I'm still dying.
Cried all I cried, but I'm still crying. Still listening to
your lying, doing my best to pretend I don't care. Tell
myself I'm done trying but look at me, I'm still there.

His Family

Watching you dream your dreams in peace, wishing I could too, wanting you to want to love me, cause all want is you - Her Love

His Family

Going from job to job, woman to woman, business to business not ever fully owning the idea of my own identity, my own dreams and desires. My life was congested with confusion. Gazing back over the shoulder of my years, laying in the shadows are the fallen corpses of ideas, efforts and endeavors that never lived to the point of fully evolved fruition. Nothing except unfinished business in spiritual matters, in business and in relationships. Misaligned illusions of probability and gambles. Not only have I done myself a deep uncensored injustice, but every person that I've had any relational connection with, they've suffered. They suffer mentally and emotionally because they're involved in a dysfunctional relationship impeded by a lack of maturity and malfunctioned through retarded functionality. I feel so dumb. I've used my gifts for any and everything but never even considered that it was given to me to be deployed into society and human service. After all this time, 45 years of living and insanely enough, I am just making attempts at exercising my gift in this life. My gift shall make room for me and I really believe that I have prolonged it long enough, but I must give honor to whom honor is due. My wife and greatest inspiration, Mrs. Tootsie Miller. If it had not been for this woman, this amazingly encouraging wife, it would not be happening now! She's sweet. She's patient, she's thoughtful, she's committed, and she loves me. This is only happening because of her pushing and coaching like I had to be when she was having the boys. I guess we switched places in the Lamaze class. She's everything. God first of course, Praise God in Jesus Name, but it is God that gave me her! Before becoming this incredible wife, she was a friendly voice of encouragement that told me from the time she met me that there was something special about me. Something different. The fact is, I couldn't see these things in myself. Still don't a lot of the time. Look, if I could be candid, I didn't have a clue as to how I was going to accomplish much of what I wanted I wanted to do in life. My perspectives were clouded, priorities misaligned from a young age, demanding the need for a competent level of multitasking that I was just not equipped with. It's stressful. It's challenging and it's humbling.

I used to write her poetry when we were dating, she loved it. I try to write a little bit now but seems I've gotten somewhat rusty over the years. Enough about me. Let me tell you about her.

She's a wonderful mother, a college graduate, a military war veteran, a nurse, a wife, a lover of God and the most beautiful person I have ever met. She is patient, understanding and kind. She cares for her home and goes above that to care for our parents because they're going into their older years. I remember the first day I was fortunate enough to talk with her. We were in AIT May of 1995, Delta 73rd Ord Battalion, Ft Gordon GA and both of us were on a restriction level they called phase. Phase was the consequence imposed if you didn't pass your physical fitness training standard, you were not allowed to leave over the weekend, and you had to be in the barracks by 10pm during the week. We weren't even supposed to be in regular civilian clothes but sometimes

His Family

we just gambled with the whole idea of it and took a chance. Anyway, she and I wound up just sitting on the steps talking. We learned a little about each other and decided to walk for a while. We walked and talked and talked some more. The rest led to us diving headlong into a full-blown relationship, where I didn't know what I was doing and neither did she. I had come into the Army from Philadelphia MS (Shout out to the P!!! ShadyOaks4Lyfe!!) and my current relationship status would not have been listed in any of those relationship status list.

My daughter's mother was pregnant and about 4 months along, wearing a ring with hopeful expectations of matrimony. We'll probably learn more about the relationship with her in **Unbreakable: The Evolving Relationship,** our debut novella where we touch on the specifics of relationships in more depth. The marriage didn't happen. That hurt her. That hurt her deeply. People use the term "forgive and forget" frequently and quite loosely.

Many times, without considerate regards for the consequential ramifications that may have fallen upon someone else emotionally or how was that person prepared to react! I hate I chose to play that period of life out like that. I may have still decided not to marry her, but I just would handle it differently now.

His Family

Tootsie was engaged to a guy that was blindsided by the fact that she and I had not only become an item, he was no longer a candidate for the husband office. From that point on, whatever life introduced to us, we dealt with it together and ironically enough, these two people who were terrible with money, came from some of the most malfunctioned of dysfunctional backgrounds, emotionally green and facing our first levels of independent freedom are still here years later. I'm thankful. We have cried, we've laughed, we had children, we cried some more, we hurt, we celebrated and after 23 years, we're still here celebrating. She has been by my side and very supportive. In fact, if I had listened to her years ago then I would be past this initial timid stage of reservation and doubt concerning writing.

One night after I had been driving the bus all day, I came home frustrated and on edge. The passengers had aggravated me and the limitations of the job itself, the way it inhibited my pressing potential had gotten the best of me. I was slowly losing clientele established during my period of barbering because I was spending all my time driving the city bus. Couldn't serve two masters. Just finishing my business degree and not understanding why I even went to college. Every time I applied for a supervisor position; I was passed over. I was disheartened and downtrodden, I just wanted her to understand. I tried my best to explain

His Family

how beat I was. How depressed and oppressed I was
feeling but instead of her understanding, she
responded, challenging me with the thing I knew
least about. "Baby write your book!" That's what
she said! The nerve, right? No, that was the mark of
a good wife. She was taken out of me and given
back to me to bring the best out of me and rightfully
so, she knew exactly what was in there! "Baby write
your book!"

That seemed like the biggest challenge, she may
as well had slapped me in front my entire neighborhood
and called me a pussy! I didn't know how. Like the thing
many women say in a condescending tone, "just be a
man!" Hell, I don't know how!

Even at my best, to let go of the comforts of a job
and the frequency that comes with a set amount of
money every week, every two weeks, how in the world
does anyone do that??? That's what she's been
challenging me to do. She recognized the true presence
of God in me reflected in the gift He has given me, and
she came along side me to push it out. I would not be
here if it was not for her dedication to us, her loyalty and
her feminine insight. I am so thankful that God didn't
give up on me and He blessed me with such an
incredible family but this woman He gave me, she's
unbreakable! I love her, and I salute her for every created
project. The writing is on the pages, the gift is on the
inside but the passion and drive, it was born in the heart
of my wife and poured on me daily. She's been my
undying inspiration.

His Family

Salute – My friend, my wife, my reason…. Mrs. Miller

Without you, none of this would be possible

His Family

Crush

Two extreme calamities. Undeniably
irresistible, whispering to the man in me.
Intensely intimate, yet untouched. Playing with
fire flirtatiously, yet not much. Encountered
countless personalities, still not such; confound
and enamored with your tender expression.

Debating mentally, am I arrested by your
words, solely in definition? Or is this
captivation my preoccupation with the ways
you move your lips when you say whatever you
say? Say something - anything. I'm listening.
Keep quiet and close your eyes - imagine this,
I'm kissing. The stanza to poems I have not
written. You're the array of bright colors in the
butterfly's wing. You're the melodic
harmonious underscore to every love-song I
sing. I made a playlist that describes our
lovemaking. Looking in your eyes, I feel your
legs shaking. Folding your body in half, gentle
back breakings, painful, but you don't mind.
Losing track of time trying to color inside the
lines or make puzzle pieces fit in a picture that
doesn't make sense. Lathered in sticky
descriptive positions, chocolate drizzled with

His Family

cherries on top. Unforgettable fantasizing about the sweetest forget-me-nots

His Family

Broken

Brokenness created insecurity.
My hurt came from the demonic voices
inside that kept luring me.
I chose to follow my own choices.

The shame of what has passed,
the discomfort of what's to come,
the disappointment of what is now living
in the deeds of what's been done.

There is no soundness in me!
There are no demons, only me.
Filled with unbelief and issues
I never took time to see

His Family

Everything is Nothing

*Stranded on islands of nothingness. A lonely peril
existence. Here dealing with this. Had a good life, now
I'm dealing with this.
Nothing from nothing leaves nothing.*

*In a time-zone with bad timing. Our love shook hands
with the hands of time now nobody can find me. I'm
nobody to nobody and everybody reminds me but I'm
nothing to you. That's why I'm sitting here with this
meaningless view. Staring into a plentiful skyline of
nothingness.*

*Arrested in incarcerated thinking. What happened in my
evolution, missing the missing link. Thinking with my
manhood, imagine what I think. Wind up with my
manhood covered in something pink. Pink cookies that
mean nothing*

*Broke down on the side of a road not often traveled.
Mind playing mind games, mentally unraveled. Not
focused or determined, mentally unprepared. Stranded
inside this nothingness with nothing everywhere*

His Family

Another Failed Male

*These blistering memories I'm remembering rape my
mind and paralyze my soul. Creep inside my innocent
unexpectedness, taking hold and won't let go. Wrestling
and fighting with all my might because all I want is to be
free. Worn down, tired from trying for so long figuring
finally, maybe that's just me.*

*All I am is failure. My black woman is right. This black
man ain't good for shit, you're better off going white.
After every attempt to be better than before, I still just
can't get right. Then hearing you say "I knew it" nails the
coffin door shut tight. My skin is disfigured. My very
existence dismembered, still all I am is a nigger.*

*At this point, I'm only a child support check to prove I
can be consistent. Our child gets excited when the check
comes, that's how she knows dad's in existence. I failed
at life by failing to live and now every new day is a
chore. Hear words that motivate others to try but I have
nothing to try for. I have no reason to live, and even
nothing more to die for. So, I live in an empty obscured
despondence holding onto past regret, reminded by the
ones that loved me most of this failure I'll never forget.*

His Family

I came across images of her.
Draped in her immaculate flowing white gown;
Her face seemed so angelic in its perfection.
I became paralyzed by the splendor of her eyes,
Mesmerized by her grace
I pondered how glorious it must've felt kneeling there
before God and her; preparing to walk forward into
forever together.

Suddenly I realized that moment would never be ours
I would never know the taste of wedding cake from her
delicate fingers; I'd never enjoy a first dance as John
Legend crooned in the background our sons would never
escort our mothers to light the unity candles

No endless photo sessions. No decadent reception
No toss of her garter and no bouquet. No happily ever
after. I've planned it in my mind a million times
Yet this day will never be. These occasions are meant for
better men; I guess that's just not me.

"Wedding Day" by Anton Cole

Artwork by Johnathan "Cool B" Brand

His Family

The Break-Up

Walked to the corner store today for a breath of fresh air, needed the exercise too. Grabbed a beer and some peanut M & M's, I can't stop thinking about you.

Came back to binge watch SVU, that's what you always watched. Netflix and chill in this house alone, now that's all that I got.

Keep checking my phone, no missed calls, no emails, and no text. No inbox on Instagram, Facebook or Twitter, no nothing. Wonder what's next?

Looked through the closet at the clothes hanging there, in a hurry you left them behind. I remember the last time you wore this dress. This whole thing's messing with my mind.

The end of the road, there was no making up. Both decided we'd done all we could do. Still, I'm staring at your clothes, watching SVU, drinking this brew, still thinking of you.

His Family

Nudge in the Night

Wake up. Wake up so I can love you. Wake up so I can candy coat your candy-coated lips. Cover and saturate them in thick candy-coated drips. Wake up so I can touch with a touch that feels like this. Wake up to taste my kiss against your candy-coated lips. Wake up!

The nights darkness grabbed my throat, tried it's best to suffocate me. My breath was shortened, I think I died, kiss me anyway. Write your forgotten forget-me-nots on the cold flesh of my corpse. Embalm me with your love, let death takes its course.

Make us happily ever after. I died at night in love with a lover I cannot have. Painfully aggravated by the echoes of her laugh. Please wake up. Not sure it even matters, not sure if you know. I poured myself inside you and I'll never let u go. I gripped you with the forceful hands of a once in a lifetime love.

Arrested you. You're mine. Brain washed and hypnotized now I've died because I've realized you can't hear me in this darkness. My cry is just too far, your sleep is way too deep, you don't hear what I need or what these crying eyes can see. It's too dark to see but you feel it all inside, you probably won't admit it cause you feeling all your pride. I understand. It's complicated but I love you anyway. I don't mind dying, take my life; let your heart be my grave. I don't mind living after death, an occurrence necessary. I only mind this detachment. Loving a lover, I can't have.

His Family

Severed from the umbilical cord of affection, craving your tender nurture, desiring that connection. If only you knew CPR and had special magic powers, you could fix the broken pieces. Touch me and release me from the grip of deaths grand finale. Please wake up.

****Boost: Love honestly. Love one person and never let anyone or anything pull your attention away from that love. ****

His Family

Was Still Born

It's likened to a newborn, maybe? My way of communicating's not communicating with you cause maybe I'm speaking "baby". Contractions and labor pains relating. I know you're there but it's so unfair because I'm the man and you're the lady. Complete miscarriage of our happy marriage.

Impregnated you with every hopeful idea I had of us and "we". Left you hoping for superman when Clark Kent was all I could be. My visions probably robbing us, short-sighted is all I see; bifocals maybe what I need? Our children have been our everything.

Our first born was our commitment, now he's gone and seems it's dying. Feel so far away from you, I'm lost, broken and crying. Men don't cry, so I hide the tears, making me broken and lying. Losing hope of making it as a couple, two people hopelessly dying.

I write the words I never say, carelessly scribbling words I watch fade away. Watch them disintegrate, dwindle, vanish and disappear. A marriage hauled away pronounced still born, suffocated by insecurity and fear.

His Family

Courtney & Corey

*How could I ever face myself? If it was a matter of
undoing mistakes, I would erase and remake myself.
Maybe life was all animated. All the imaginations and
fantasies we hoped we'd be, but never made it.*

*Don't think I even considered what I wanted to be when I
grew up. Got older, start eating wasted time until I threw
up. I made three amazing children; probably can't take
credit for that because I wasn't aiming. Now it's my
children I'm claiming. One day Snook will look me in my
eyes, she'll ask me "Daddy why?". Wasn't I even worth
your time, didn't you ever bother trying? She's always
been "Daddy's Girl", but an absent Daddy is no Daddy
at all. No matter how many letters he writes, no matter
how many times he calls.*

*No matter how many checks get sent, no matter how
much money. I'm feeling like such a dummy. I'm in a
race, been spinning my wheels steady running in place,
yelling at myself to pick up the pace. Going nowhere fast
without yall and at your age, wonder how you feel? I
can't apologize enough. I'm sorry though. Courtney,
Corey....I'm sorry though. I'm trying to be better with
Caleb; but I miss both of you. I love you. Don't know
much else to say......just I love you. If I was there right
now, I'd hug you. No words, no explanations; I'd hug
you right now*

His Family

Hopelessly Hoping

*Stuck in this place of abnormality. Abnormally
malfunctioning but it's abnormally normal to me. No one
to blame in this game being played, the choices were
made, the voices are noises that come here to stay. I wish
I could hug Courtney, she's no doubt suffering too. I
want so bad to talk to Corey; I know he's going through.
He doesn't understand much about the things he's
feeling now. I want to be there for him, but son I don't
know how. Feels like my hands are tied and my insides
have grown cold. I've given y'all bad examples. Sitting
here stewing in the rue of stabilized instability,
smothered in a gravy of shame and this pain's inside
killing me. I'm nothing. Bubbling with the aggravations
of lust and still lusting. Dying daily. Spiritual regressive
oppression and no one can save me. Tears drop like
blood to stain the pillows I sleep on. Death would be a
privilege if I fell asleep to sleep on. Just let me sleep and
sleep on. Die peacefully in quiet. Rehabilitating this
life's a waste of time, why bother trying.*

*A lost and empty man, pockets filled with regrets, heart
filled with horrible memories I always wanna forget.
Memories I want to see fall off the pages of
remembering, boiling in sinful lust without a fight so I'm
here simmering. Standing here in the middle of
indiscretion remembering the love we once had. The love
now gone bad. The wife I've mistreated that freely gave
me all her heart. Same wife that loved me more than she
loved herself from the start. Standing here thinking of
how selfish I am and how selfish I've always been.*

113

His Family

Standing here with only the hopes of hoping it all would end

His Family

Friends for Life

Mortified and numb mentally. Caught up in harsh illusions of who I thought was a friend to me. Distracted and disconnected, recklessly ignoring the signs. Every effort put forth to be a friend to him when he was never mine. I couldn't tell my secrets, he told them every time. Couldn't share my vulnerabilities, he exposed them every time. He challenged me repeatedly, times I wasn't even trying, but I didn't know we were competing. Validation wasn't important to me, that's not what I needed. We were friends for different reasons to each other's what I'm seeing. While I was wanting us to be better, a friend is not what he was needing.

Would've split my extra value meals, let him have the fries. Always let him tell the dirt he did and kept it all inside. He used to tell his girl my name and I would be his alibi. I would've given my left arm to help him reach his goal. In death, I'd give my life so my brother could keep his soul. Nothing I wouldn't have done because he means that much to me. Guess being a friend ain't something everybody's cracked up to be.

His Family

Shadow of Death

Anxiety is my closest friend. We've been together so long, we really know each other. I've held it in my bosom like she was the side piece of relief that caused dissention between me and my lover. I've grown to love her. I've learned that what I am is never good enough. I've learned that if people accept you for who you are it's only until you're not enough.

Guilty by association. Associated with judgmental prejudices that never accepted me anyway. I live a life of loneliness and exclusion. The misfit that missed the fitting session yet still wants to fit into places that teach the sickest lessons. The people that care for me the least haunt my mind when we disagree because they always wind up leaving me. Wonder if it'll ever cease. Will I ever know the privilege of community or destined to live life a lonely me.

Destined to be all I need. I'm nothing more. Mom and Dad didn't want me, I wonder what they had me for. Nothing from nothing leaves nothing. I wonder if God even cares. I wonder if all the praying's futile, I wonder if He's even there. Donned in dreadful dissatisfaction disillusioned by demented despair. In my mind's a holocaust, Hiroshima everywhere. Dead bodies and blood stains, I'm stepping over corpses. Stomping into my darkness and leaving behind my nothing more. Leaving children plagued emotionally that I didn't do nothing for. I've made them feel the pain of my inadequacy and now I'm struggling to help them find

His Family

their way. We sit at the tables for dinner and don't know what to say. I look into their eyes and I know they want some answers. Emotional bankruptcy interrupts me whenever I attempt an answer. My response is sore jilted, filled with guiltiness and hurt. I humble myself stumbling being the dad they deserve. Standing out like a sore thumb, circles getting smaller. Writing's laced with hopelessness; seems I've lost all hope for this.

Scrolled through my contacts with nobody to contact. Nobody to reach out to because nobody even knows. No family to accept me, nowhere to even go. Everybody's busy pissing in their own dilemmas until they decide to piss in my house, then they give me their agenda. Everybody calls once their pressures comes to life, trouble with their children, jobs, money, house and wife. Trouble standing adversity, cowards and counterfeits. I missed the class of fitting in but manhood's the class they missed. They have issues, they call me with the list, I'm suppose I'm a good listener because all I do is listen. Holding the phone wishing the signal would be lost. They'd have someone that they needed then who somehow dropped the call. I think about the times I never was good enough it seemed. I think of how when shit hits the fan, they somehow call on me. I think of all the jokes they had about the writing and the vision. The ones that said it'll never work, thought I'd abort the mission. Well here I am still writing, the lonely the misfit with a wish. Still fighting, still going on. Wanting to so badly to fit in but still living alone

His Family

Growing up as a young man introduces an entirely unknown share of challenges even if there's a strong male presence present. The fact that males are inherently conditioned to suppress emotions and shun thinking that may go contrary to the group thinking, retards development and stifles community cohesion. Most of what I adopted in my adolescent phases of life came from media and rap music's' portrayal of what a strong resilient black male is supposed to look like. You got to be tough, slang guns and don't take no shit. That's the perception of the average male. More importantly, you got to get lots of women. Have sex with as many as you possible could and make them enjoy the fact that you gave them the opportunity to be with you that way. Behavior that results in STD's, teen pregnancy and dislocated father figures also keep the revolving wheels of degenerative dysfunction spinning. Sounds ridiculous right? It is, but the reality of it remains the same. This repetitive cycle continues to cycle young men through a deliberately programmed way of thinking that inhibits us from our youth. It's not altogether color specific, but it is about the numbers that can be affected by the deficiency. So, you'll see where some of this is touched on in the next piece.

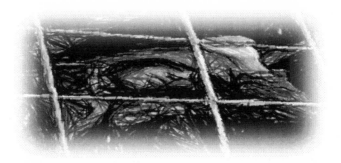

The Hood of Manhood

Manhood does man no good unless there's a respect for that manhood from the men in the man's hood. Something about being gangster makes a man more influential. The more revered he will be and feel, the more people he cheats and kills. There must be violence. There must be a mindset that speaks, "I will not let you mess over me"! There must be an understanding that that's the way he's supposed to be. That's who he is intended to be and if a man is not that, then that man is not a man at all, where are the real men at? The fanciest car, most expensive clothes and big bank rolls to flash. Women say they can be happy without money but then only want men with cash. Only want men that will beat a man down if the other man disrespects her. He packs a Glock 40 and is not scared to use it when it comes a time to protect her. Now he's locked up. She finds another man.

His Family

Manhood should never show weakness, it's not cool, to cry at death's view. We walk around harboring these feelings until the point we don't know what to do.

Our entertainment is carnage. UFC and dog fights, the more blood, then the better. The blood drips at our door, we wonder what for and ask ourselves when will things get better. Antagonistic lives challenge us daily leaving us to question our worth. Vulnerability is not acknowledged; emotions are off limits because that's what we're taught from our birth. "You stop that crying! Crying's for punks!" are the words that infected our souls. So, in zombie like fashion we adopt our impressions and portray them continually until we're old. White suburban emulate blacks, blacks emulate Italians, so the cycle gets bigger and bigger. Masculinity is determined by the size of the gun and not the character of the finger on the trigger. "Squeeze nigga! wait, No justice! No peace!", is the chant we hear in the streets, but we can't cry for justice while unjust we continue to be.

Incarceration or Caskets, the violent mind's thought out the course. If the only response is violence and the consequence is force, then the solution we strive for is the identical twin to the source. Violence begets violence and to prove we never scared, there must be retaliation. Simple minded Neanderthal club over the head, the bigger club is the voice of the Nation.

His Family

Only the strong survive, but what really measures strength? Is it the muscles the mind or the myth? What measures yours must be what measures mine so is it the God, the giver or is it the gift? The boys in the hood are always hard but inside they're still just boys. Filled with contention and calamity of confusion and equating heroism to noise.

Usually the one talking is the one saying the least and not even much value in what's said. So historically he's the first one on the floor bleeding, the first to get bust in the head. The bigger they are the harder they fall so the tall tree hits the ground hardest. Lays there the longest so spectators can see that the first one to fall's the one started it.

I have failed in relationships, friendships and life but manhood wouldn't let me stay down. If you find male resilience willing to stand for their family, then that's where the male strength is found. If we see it in honesty, brotherhood and integrity then there's a clearer example to see. If I see it in you and you see it in him, I'll respect him while you respect me. I'll respect all your efforts while you struggle thru life understanding you're doing what you can. Hopefully, I can help you and if I need it, help me, understanding that's what we do as a man!

His Family

A Man of My Word

*Words can be consolation,
used to tell you how I feel.
Words examined can help
distinguish what's fake from
what's real. Words can
provide security explaining
how much I love you still.
My words have come to
comfort, my words are here
to heal.*

*My words came to affirm,
build you up on every side.
To replace your bouts of
doubt and leave
encouragement inside. My
words will never hurt you,
they'll soothe & satiate. I'll
use words to make you smile
and lift off heavy weights.*

*My words will meet
emotional voids where
others have always failed to.
If you ever feel like you're in
this alone, I'll be right there
to tell you. It's my word, I'll
never fail you.*

Now to be a man of my word

His Family

Outer Darkness

I find myself at a loss for words! What kind of writer loses the knack for his "knick knack patty whack?" I wish you would, I wish I could.... If there was some cause for the pause, I would not need recall the calls and the letters and the "things will get better" but who am I? Where are we?

Who is this monster I've become? Why am I still here and no use to anyone? Why have my fears come alive singing songs that leave me confused? Misused and abused, yet the only one here for me right now is the one I'm about to lose. Why? Such a lonely existence and such an intense resistance. Writing line on top of line leaves me at a loss for words then at unexpected times, I write things I've never heard! This lonely life's so absurd.

Intelligence misappropriated is intelligence unassociated, for some a battle they can't win. Knowing the right thing to do and doing the best thing for you that opposes the right thing, is still sin. My friend where art thou? Where is this place that I cry and search for? What is true love and why do I constantly crave more? My heart is a vacuum sucking life out of others. If I'm on life support don't let me recover! Let my pillow of comfort be the same one that smothers, then let me die of suffocation. Detach me from life to set this world free of animation and disassociate this discontent from my own disassociation.

His Family

Are you kidding? This is not a game and I know I can't win, I lost in the beginning and now I'm losing here in the end. Bottom of the ninth. Bases loaded...where do I turn? Where do I go?

His Family

Classmate

*Don't even know you but you're beautiful; unfolding
time lives in your eyes. Forced to sit across from you
trying not to imagine what's inside. The tone your voice
projects. Who's responsible for your being? How could
words describe this indescribable beauty sitting across
from me I'm seeing. Held captive magnetically by this
gorgeous misleading that just won't set me free. Trapped
in desire while sitting across from you at this table and
you can't see me.*

*Ooooops! My eyes hit yours and now I'm reluctant to
look up again. This child-like infatuation giving me that
"can't get enough again".*

*You had to be drawn on the canvas of universal
constellations with star studded angelic detail. Designed
penmanship coupled with femininity, now I'm across the
table from you today when tomorrow, you won't
remember me. Tomorrow you'll be a memory, I'll be
desiring you still. A few hours we walk away from this
table to go wherever we will.*

*To feel whatever, we feel and be whoever we are.
Wonder if you'll remember me when you get wherever
you are? Think of me right there where you are.*

*You've inspired me from across this table by giving a
beauty I could see. If you glance at my paper while I'm
sitting here scribbling, you'll know I'm glad you sat
across from me.*

His Family

Want (Explicit)

I wanna do more than touch you, I wanna become your senses. I want to be there when you feel alone, feel me moving in your skin. I want to do more than taste you, I wanna become your taste. Every time you swallow you feel me moving in your face. Imagine that. Imagine me. Imagine closing your eyes to see. Imagine falling apart in pieces and remembering a broken heart. Imagine piecing it back together to be stronger than the hurtful part. It doesn't hurt anymore. I have you in my life, so he really doesn't flirt anymore unless you're not around. Imagine when it first slides inside you and you make that lovemaking sound. Imagine fucking me slowly while I whisper for you to hold me; afterwards I choke you because I don't want love. I just want to watch you die in my arms and wonder what you were made of. Wonder what's happily ever after with all the glitz and bling. Wonder if there's a happy place in love where all the lovebirds sing. I wonder if tomorrow you'll even there for me be. I even wonder if there's an us and I imagine what we could be.

His Family

Inside You (Explicit)

I want to be inside you. It's raining, I feel so alone. I scrolled thru my contacts with no one to contact and I'm in the car with nowhere to be. Counting the raindrops, adjusting A.C. and thinking about you and about me. Really thinking about us wondering why you're not here. Wondering if I could be good to you if you were near. Wondering would you leave him, and would I leave her, or would we just fuck and leave things like they were.

Raindrops. The rain stopped but the windshield's still wet, the remnant still lingers like your cream from your tender body drips from my fingers. What's left is still there just like memories of us. I want the details of your life. Let me love you like a wife; you love me like a husband. In fact, love me better and leave that love shit for your husband. Love me better, love me harder and always finish what you start so if we started long ago it seems that we're not finished yet. We have new memories to remember and promises to not forget.

You'll be my best love yet and I'll be your "happily ever after". Even now in the stillness of the blowing A.C., I can hear your laughter. Always smile and think of me, always be by my side. Always kiss me and grab this dick, push me deep inside. I want to be inside you.

His Family

A Man

Familiar to a man's heart's the gleam of his inner dream. All he's ever seen is everything that could ever seem. Highly esteemed is his toil and treasure measured by his possessions. Left to love a world of sin, he cleaves to misdirection.

His mind holds understanding, moving him through dark uncertainty to face his own demands. Against the winds of opposition, he positions himself and stands, listening to resolve, doing all he can.

An Unopened Book

Staring at blank screens and empty pages. Lost and confused daily in heartaches and contemplations. Wasn't my intention to make us face this thing we're facing but we're facing it still.

No guidance, no direction just doubts and disappointments. Painful words of remembrance and to write them is my ointment. Who God calls He qualifies, so why am I anointed? My life's congested with hoes and money, guns, drinking and smoking joints. What's the point?

My hurt is deeper than I'll ever tell, plus no one wants to hear. I push people away that care for me when I only want them near. Accustomed to lies and abandonment,

His Family

childhood filled with fear. Smiling and cracking jokes to hide a crying heart filled with tears.

The more I look inside myself, reliving the hurt I've caused; the way I broke the hearts of others it wasn't their fault at all. Now I pray to God and call Him hoping one day He'll hear me. For now, I'm staring into the soul of my life, blank pages are all I see

His Family

You'll Never Know

*The guilty stare of this benign
impulse gazing thru my soul
reminded me of us, but they're
not there anymore. We held
hands forever, now it's been
forever since we let go. All we
have now are smoke filled
places where our smiles use to
be. I have pictures of you and
I'm sure you have pictures of
me but I'm deleting a few more
each day. As real as my
imagination made us, I knew in
my heart you weren't there to
stay. I knew you couldn't stay
around so once I cry myself a
river then I'll jump in and
drown because you're gone. I
know what it means to be
lonely but never felt so all
alone. My ravaged carcass
being eaten with pains inside
my bones.*

His Family

I wish we'd never met to create all these dreadful memories I'm wishing I could forget. Forget your kiss, forget your smile, forget your touch, the things you do; forget about forgetting things then maybe forget about you. The more pictures I delete, the more the thoughts of you linger. Seems even when I don't hear from you, I still feel you in my fingers, so I type. You're just my type. You're just right but I hate that you're not here. I'm afraid I've lost you forever, now I forever live in fear. Dreadful reality, a lifetime fallacy. Take time to remember me and when you're reading, think of this.... wait, my pride won't let me send it, so you'll never know how much you're missed

His Family

I'm feeling alone in my own mind. My thoughts keep me company, but I'm so lost. Deserted by affection on the island of abandon. "Why me?" is what I ask but nobody ever answers when I'm asking. A forgotten past. Wish I could kiss the pain goodbye and painlessly say goodbye at last.

Wind up French kissing memories, the kiss of death remembers me. I feel alone. Distant emotionally. Downtrodden and despondent. Calling all my contacts but nobody's responding. In fact, a phone full of contacts but nobody to contact. If only they knew? If only the tinted windows of my soul would let light shine through. If only I could look in the mirror and not have to see this dude.

Mental abuse. Wounded because of the selfish paths I chose. Calgon take me away! Let me live to fight another day. Fought the demons all my life but now it seems they're here to stay. How do I fight what I can't see? Why would I strive for what I can't be? Is life a possibility? How do I fight what I can't see? How do I defeat what's only me?

His Family

Alone Time

*She reached to make love to me, I just wanted to sleep.
She wanted us to spend time together, but I just wanted
to creep. She needed me to be a man that I refused to be.
Now I'm here in this lonely place, nobody here but me.*

*We could've gone to higher heights, I just wouldn't
reach. Made her attempt to live a beautiful life with the
ugliest parts of me. Made her wonder if things were bad,
would I be there like she needs. Now I'm wondering from
this lonely place, nobody here but me.*

*Said "women all have attitudes", that I still believe. But
what would you do if you gave him your heart and all he
gave was grief? What would you do if you fucked him
good and all he did was cheat? What would you do if
you gave him your all, then he decided to leave?*

*Yes, women have attitudes and in part I know why. She's
stuck dealing with the consequences of a man that
wouldn't try. Seen this happen most my life, no way I
could lie. Guilty of the same behavior, there is no getting
by.*

*Its hard cause I love women, but this one means so much
to me. I try to give her all I have, be everything she
needs. It boils down to not doing what we feel; but doing*

133

His Family

what she need. Too bad it took this time alone for me to even see.

Fairytale Love

*Your affection intoxicates
me. Do what you feel. Do
whatever you will.... just
don't stop. I just don't
want u to stop.*

*Give me a love that never
ends, an intimate
intertwining that forever
transcends the
distinctions of space and
time. Stare in the eyes of
your forever and tell me
you'll be forever mine.
See if we're together, I'll
be forever fine cause
truly all I need is you. So
just do what you do but
don't stop.*

*Let me be your forget-
me-nots. You be my wish
upon a star. Then maybe
I can twinkle-twinkle just
to be right where you are
or is it all a fairy tale.*

His Family

*If so, I'm happily ever
after just holding your
hand, making you laugh
and listening to your
laughter. You made my
morning. You're the
sunshine that I see. Now
whatever you wanna be,
baby you can be that with
me*

His Family

Are You My Lover?

Are you my lover? Born from the other side of a dark heaven, clothed in sensual hallucinations. Plausible oxymorons are the cause of my frustration so I contemplate the contemplations. Consider the moisture of your kiss. The blackness in loves dying leaves all the lovers crying and all the honest men lying but through the thick fog of painful ecstasy, I still feel you next to me and I whisper.... "Are you my lover?"

Abandonments torture bodies embodied in erotic everlastings. Mummified incandescent fragments of fragmented memories. Come to me my love, if thou be my lover in truth. Are you my lover indeed? Then do as a lover must do. Come into my darkness. Die this blissful death. Submit yourself completely surrendering all that you have left. Bow yourself before me. Kneel now at my feet. Let fragrant brush strokes of your hairbrush me everywhere and tell me...are you my lover?

Are you indeed my lover? Witches awe in amazement! Let the dead masturbate dripping drops of blood all over you. Let death lick you in your hidden places then ravish you the way lovers do. Come bow thyself before me, acknowledging yesterday's farewell and render thyself unto me making this day kiss and tell. Let this day guide you gently, darkness touch you like no other. Die with me in love making, if thou truly be my lover. Are you my lover?

Dream Girl

A soft hand to hold; good company is what we are as this love story unfolds. A tank top and panties, the suggested scratch for my itch. She turns me on with no switch. Ignites burning flames inside my body and never strikes the match. Fires burn intensely. Yearn for her immensely.

Would love to wish upon a star but knowing that's not real, so I wish upon a million flickering constellations hoping wishes come true still. Hope she knows just how I feel and how I light up when she laughs. I hope she understands that she's the best thing I've ever had and will never have.

Light brown eyes stare at me ripping thru my timid core, finding the reality of the man in me that she's always waited for. I'm here waiting for you too, that's what lovers do. They take time with their lives to exist, breathe and thrive in a world of imagination. Loving intimate anticipation curled up with expectation and lying next to sheer seduction. Reluctantly knowing where this is never going but still willing to go, go there with her still. Nowhere found to build a hiding place from affections unexpected lure, can't believe that this endured the test of time.

Sands flow thru the glass and they're never seen again but she flows thru me like DNA, I see her in my skin. She's a part of me. Almost the very heart of me but the constant thumping of my inner life muscle reminds me....

His Family

she's not there. I say goodnight and the next morning there's no pill to remedy what last night feels. She's gone. It was all a dream and the girl of my dreams was never real.

His Family

Hidden Fantasy

Can I hide you in my fantasy? Not to misuse your femininity, but let you have your way with the man in me. Open the doors of my insanity and let you walk in first. Listen to your pains, making the best of what was your worse. Sightseeing thru all our memories and putting our good times in reverse so the good becomes better. Let my kisses make you better. Let's kiss like this together. I hope missing me makes you wetter. I want you wet for me.

Everything we encounter causes a physical response, so how do you respond to me? How do I respond to you? How would you even want me to, what would you want to do? Touch me. Never mind. This is not the place, now is not the time but I'm there and I know you feel me. Intellectual intimacy, I let you touch the real me. Do you like the way that feels?

I'm not letting you go, refuse to love you less. I'm not leaving you insecure. I see nothing but the best and I see that in you. I see a beauty in you that you probably don't see yourself. Let me resuscitate your desires after you take your last breath. After you die your last death and there's nowhere for you to be, I'd breathe into your lifeless corpse to bring you back to me. I'd hide you in my fantasy.

His Family

I really would kiss you. The kiss of unspoken things in a language only you and I can understand, I really should. Let my words drip all over your lips and trust me, I really would. Sometimes I get carried away. Sometimes it's more alluring to carry you off in your thoughts. What are you thinking? Poetry can be so many things. Poetry can change the mood if we only allow it to. Let poetry touch you. Let poetry change you. Let the words uncover you and discover your inhibitions. Your body whispers softly, that's when poetry listens.

Don't Touch Me

I love to touch you with my mind. Touch you, touch you, touch.... I love when you touch me and not feel me (that's borrowed), but still true. I crave the touching touch from you. Ideas become figments of lust-filled imaginations, inanimate desires move to mental penetrations and that's me. Me inside you inside me inside you, that's me. We don't pause, stop, or hesitate because I'm touching you. I absolutely looooove to touch you with my mind then I find that in time, I blush. A child-like smirk born in the stables of shy obscenities, intimate conceptions only a reflection of what happened previously, it started because I wanted to touch you more. Let my touch explain what your body's made for.

Your mind takes new focus, things appear the same; it's one view, one perception, one idea, one you, one me and all we see is the way I touch you. Relax most beautifully adored, I'm here for your pleasure, relax. There is no right or wrong only you, only me and our all night long enveloped in desire. I love to touch you with my mind until you shake and cringe, impulses all over your soft tender loins. Until you breathe deep and pour drops of creamy rain, covering my outer limits. Do we have limits? If so then let's move past them but first, let me touch you with my mind. Until....well, let me touch you there lightly, then my deliciously flavored damsel you utterly become with infinite ease the poem which I do not write. Just let me touch you with my mind

His Family

****Boost: Good sexual chemistry happens even when you're not engaged in the act of sex. It's chemistry. Just let the fire burn***

His Family

Beautiful (Explicit)

Once upon a time in an enchanted experience, there lived a starving expression of a woman named beautiful. Tortured by routine and normalcy, she felt shackled and chained in expectation, in uncertainty when all she wanted was to be touched. To be felt. To live in lust and know what's left because there had to be more. She needed to be fucked until her tender pussy was sore then fucked some more.

Fairy tales turn me on. I hear your name in the words of every song. I fall asleep wanting to hold you all night long but it's all fairy tale. Subconsciously unconscious. I read old messages or imagined the next time because the last time is never our last time, you'll always be mine. Do you mean that? You lie so much.

Inside this beauty of a woman is a story left untold so I'm listening eagerly to learn what part she plays. Speaking of playing.... let's slip my fingers inside you. You lay on your tummy reaching back to feel me slipping inside you. Face parts your ass cheeks and tongue wetting your ass, finger fucking you slow. Squeeze your breast. Harder. Stop reading and really squeeze like I would. Like I do. Look in my eyes, hypnotize me, seduce me like I'm you. Harder....feel me all thru your body. I'm consuming you. We can stop if you like but I won't let you.

His Family

*I don't remember your name but how could I ever
forget your laughter. That's right, your name's
Beautiful, and they lived happily ever after*

Lost in Thought (Nighttime)

*3am having flashbacks. Reminiscing over things I'm
missing and the things I can never have back. You were
giving me all I wanted but telling me I couldn't have that,
now I'm missing you. Laying here wide awake,
imagining kissing you. I'm here all alone. Flipping thru
old messages in my phone like I can hear your voice.
Silent thoughts of you killing me while all I hear is noise.
Goodnight*

His Family

One is a voice of love a lover hears in the night hours. The other, the uncontrollable head-locked mentality of reasoning that takes control of the mind anywhere at any time. The unhampered thought. It's daydreaming. The voice that cannot be blocked no matter how hard you try. Love doesn't respect locations or occupations. Uninhibited, uncensored desire. No matter how hard you want to shake the feelings and not be in love with a person, it's just not that easy. Especially when it's all over, everything's out of your control and they have moved on with their lives. The last thing they want is to deal with or hear what you're thinking. So, I wrote it all out....

His Family

Lost in Thought (Daytime)

What am I thinking about? About you, about me. About what we are, what we've been and all of what we'll be. About everything we used to be. About the things we've looked forward to, all the things we can't see. I'm thinking that love is blind, perhaps it's a loving cataract. Distorted vision blurrily impaired by the things we counteract. One misinterpreted lie can keep a love affair intact, but this is true. The truest me for the truest you. The truest black for the truest blue and we call it midnight. A kiss when the clock strikes twelve turns your carriage back to pumpkins. Leaves secret lovers searching for something. Always in two places brokenhearted without each other. Hoping she knows he loves her. Hoping his love will smother the breath from any air of doubt. There's always someone loving her, she'll never be without. He's there. Right there. Right there loving you....

His Family

****Boost: Don't let new beginnings discourage you!
You already know how to start this time. Remember,
there's a difference in starting over and starting
again!****

The soul desires tasting.
Teeth sinking, a piercing
bite catapulting them into
an eternal intertwined design.

The vampires wine.
The never-ending of time.
Desire; the soul's desire to
be consumed by a lover's pain.

He drinks the blood of her passion,
now she'll never be the same

His Family

Kiss Goodbye

Something broke our frame of forever. Tore down our called always and brought an end to the never-never, in this desolate never-never land of love we always treasured. A beautifully painted rendition; thought we'd be together forever. At least, that's the way the story ended in this book I read once.

Now the everything is nothing, the cusp of always has come to this. Our kisses goodbye say goodbye when kissing goodbye without a kiss. I lost my virginity in a meaningless drunken indiscretion. That girl doesn't speak to me now and that's so painful. I've been living to manipulate women since then, that's painful. Shameful even.

Never imagined hurting you this way. Sitting here full of words with nothing left to say. Crying out to God with nothing left to pray so I just jot down words rambling. Hoping these words reach you while this broke gamblers gambling. There's nothing else I know. No smile smiling back, no hand to hold. No way for me to hold you close, memories are all I know. Hurt all that ever loved me, so I'm loving letting you go.

His Family

Shame

*I felt myself slipping, but this shame wouldn't let me
reach. There has always been someone to help, my pride
wouldn't let me see. Wanted to be perfect, imperfections
wouldn't let me be but then again, it's all perception. A
matter of how we see.*

*Sought love in other places, left my own home to die.
Reasoned everything was lost, not even worth a try.
Found myself entangled in a weakness I never respected.
A part of me that's haunted me all my life, but I
neglected. The part of manhood no man wants to admit
so we reject it and rejection is what I did. Felt just like a
little kid that broke a glass while washing dishes then hid
all the broken pieces hoping momma never missed it.
Soon as they get home she always goes right to the
kitchen and ask, "what happened to that glass?". I'm
standing there scared as hell, can't believe she asked.*

*It's silence. Internal truth colliding. The lie you hiding
reacting violently with convictions on the inside. I lied.
"Are you cheating on me?" Needless to say, I lied. I'm
so ashamed I played this game but even more than that,
I'm ashamed that I believe this is all I am and where I'm
at. I'm ashamed that I don't feel I can commit to being
loved. See I can give it away, but it's not something I'm
worthy of. I'm so ashamed*

His Family

The Parking Lot: A Short Story

"Can we stop by the store really quick; I promise it'll only take a minute. There are some things we need around the house and if we stop now, I can run in and get them. You can wait out in the car", that's what my wife said I could do. That's what I was thinking the whole time she was talking; I was just making sure she knew. I could do some reading, maybe some writing or catch up on a new album that's out. It was six in the evening the parking lots packed at the store, there's no way I'm getting out. Get Out? Get it? Anyway, I let the seat back, turned the music up a little and closed my eyes just for a second. Not more than 10 minutes and then I heard barking, certainly not what I expected. I raised up, looked around, the barking got louder so I grew more curious than before. Got out the car and followed the sound to a couple cars over from the Explorer. Someone had gone inside in apparently a hurry and left the pooch locked up inside. The AC was running so the pup was okay but all the people walking made him excited. The lot was so full and seemed everyone was rushing in total disregard for each other, then I heard another noise, certainly wasn't a dog barking, sounded more like some lovers. "Yea, Yea baby! Oooooo baby, it's so good" were the words I could hear and I'm looking to find where they came from. Then spotted a car with foggy windows, legs in the air inside and from the sounds of her, she's about to cum. The car was bouncing and rocking right here in the lot, seems the people inside gave it all that they got. Seems they lost track of the

His Family

place they were in and couldn't wait to get home, they wanted it right then. I stared at the car and wanted bad to walk over, peep inside the window until it was over. Enjoy just spectating but I saw unmarked cars. Police on the lot not too far from where we are. Not sure what they were doing but they weren't too concerned about the people who were screwing. It's something else they're pursuing.

Me, I'm steady glued to the car that's still rocking and the legs in the air while she's taking his cock until I heard a soft cry of a baby close by in a car with the windows up locked up inside. I didn't mind the pooch because the car was still running but this child was trapped inside this hot car without their mommy. Locked up inside this hot car without the dad while the parents were inside, this shit was making me mad. Her skin color was changing, her little cry was slight and weak, so I ran inside to have them call the parents to the scene. Gave them the license number and the car's full description, then waited for someone to rush to the front so I could whoop 'em. People want children, someone would love this one and they're crying for you in the car while you go about your business. Minutes passed, and I thought about the police in the lot. Hurried outside and jogged to the spot I saw the cops. Tapped on the window and they wouldn't let it down to talk to me. I tapped some more until he finally opened the door. I tried explaining but I guess my nervousness seemed aggressive. The officer told me I was interfering with police business. He asked to see my ID and ask was I on drugs. I was dressed very

His Family

casual guess he assumed I was a thug. I tried
cooperating, by giving them my ID card, he asked was
the address right and got back in the car. Suppose they
ran my license while I kept standing there, the door
opened in the car that had the legs up in the air. Two
people got out happily and both happened to be
grinning; fixing their clothes to my surprise, both were
women. Nevertheless; not my worry, get back to this
child. The officer got out slowly after being there for a
while. He finally listened to me and beckoned for his
partner, then we all walked to the car that wasn't very
far. The windows hot to the touch and the baby had
stopped crying. Her skin looked very flush, "Oh my God
I think she's dying! Sir you have to open the door!" The
officer said, "I'm trying!" Then push me out the way,
told me get out his face. Treated me like the criminal
with apparent distaste included. I'm thinking" Why's he
such a jerk and what'd I do to you?" They finally went to
the other side to break the glass and get inside, but just
before the glass broke, a voice spoke. That's the parent
apparently. Rushing over with the keys and all of this is
scaring me. No way to prepare for what's happening
today, there's no comparing. The whole time this
emergency unfolds, this cop's steady staring. Car opens,
reached for the child who probably will not live. She's
nonresponsive. No ambulance, no CPR to give. The
police tried everything, but the little baby had died, my
eyes filled up with tears even though I knew I tried.
"Why?" is all I ask. What's so important in the store?
The ambulance finally pulled up quietly, I don't know
what for. They took the little baby and put her on

153

His Family

machines, then after a couple of attempts, pronounced her dead on the scene. My wife walks out the store to find me, face all wet with tears. The officer says, "move along folks, nothing to see here". They ask would I give a statement. I said "no", not knowing the bother, the statement won't bring this baby back and you could've tried a little harder. We all could've saved this babies life if we weren't caught up in ourselves. If we were more aware of what was going on than our minds caught somewhere else. We walked to the car, wife said she would drive, backed up and pulled away. The officer waved his hand flagging us down, guess he has something else to say. I'm completely lost at this point so I'm about to fall asleep. Whatever he wants, my wife could answer so he doesn't need to talk to me. I couldn't shake the look of that lifeless little body, the way it flopped when they lifted her. Couldn't shake the fear of me frantically running finding where the parents were. I couldn't explain it, I just wanted to pass out. Go home, relax and retire. Car comes to a stop and this sorry ass cop gave us a ticket; the tags were expired! Ain't that a bitch!

His Family

Mind Games

Disoriented insanity. Vulnerability of the mind has been crushed by calamity. Scared. Unprepared. Lacking mental dexterity. Taking steps but still standing and standing still is scaring me. Not ready to move forward and not prepared for what's preparing me.

Problematic, sifting thru fuzzy muddled muffled noises. Even in sorting out the choices I can still hear the voices. The unreasonable suggestions call me signifying I should set flames to myself. Blame my pain for this shame but this shameful pain's all I have left. Self-inflicted wounds, response unpredictable. I'm feeling the pain of failing more and more with passing time. Perhaps I had to feel this pain to gain some peace of mind.

His Family

Little Faith

Stop staring at my fear,
tampering with this weakness.
Don't make me whimper words in silence,
my feelings don't feel like speaking.

Don't gauze this heart hemorrhaging
bleeding should it cease from beating.
Don't attempt to mend my unbelief,
you don't have all the pieces.

Don't! Don't! Just Don't! Leave now, Just Go!

Don't you talk to me about healing,
you can't understand my wounds.
Don't talk about being born again
you can't push me in the womb.
Don't suggest I find the bride;
I ain't fit to be a groom.
Life abundantly is not worth living,
looking forward to the tomb.

Not that I don't want to heal,
too ashamed to remove the cover.
Easy to say you love me now,
you don't know this obscured lover

Soon to be Released Sneak Peek

"The Wooden Spoon"

Bottles, pampers, extra jar of baby food, wipes, clean diaper clothes were just a few of the items I was struggling to remember packing that morning. Being a new mommy, I tried to imagine every scenario and like any young mother, found myself wrestling with the wondering if I was being a good mother. Moving hurriedly from the dresser to the bed where my handsome Babyboy was, then to the bathroom, then back to the dresser, "Lord, what am I forgetting?" I kept asking, while fidgeting with the three pair of earrings, contemplating which set to wear today. You were just three-weeks old, and I had you dressed in the cutest little sailor suit with a matching white beret, and little white baby shoes with navy strings to match the highlight of the outfit. You had just been changed so anybody that picked you up, would see a poof of white powder from the heavy hand of baby powder I just dumped inside your underclothes. I used petroleum jelly to slick your hair, face arms and legs, you was ready. I had you so shiny when you was a baby. You were such a good boy too. You would just lay there kicking your little chubby legs and laughing. If yo pamper was clean, you was happy and content watching the ceiling fan blades spin and making gurgling noises. Such a good baby, didn't cried much at all so that gave me all the time in the world to move around freely, getting dressed. With you being so young, it wasn't likely that you would roll off the bed because you had not developed much up to this point and the queen-sized bed would require you roll at least three times before you were at the edge. I combed my hair to pull it back in a bun. Now you know ya momma ain't never been no ugly girl. Back then, I was very pretty, still am if I must say so myself. Caramel skin,

Soon to be Released Sneak Peek

prominent facial features and voluptuous top front made me the real eye catcher to most young men. I step out with all these boobs and guys would break they necks looking. Most college girls longed for that attention, but not me. I was quiet, reserve, chaste if you will. Your auntie would always say I was a wallflower, whatever that means. Nevertheless, seemed the shyness made me more attractive. I was a slight bit on the heavy side. In high school, the boys would make fun of me and call me fatty or big girl. Ignorant. I had to learned to ignore the immature scoffs but could hardly fight off the belief I developed about myself. You know, after you hear something for so long, if you're not careful, you will start to believe it. All the insults from the young boys made it difficult to see the pretty girl that everybody else called me later. I saw fat and ugly. I saw disgusting and unattractive. I saw someone nobody would ever dream of loving. Even in the mirror, when the person looking back at me would tell me these horrible things about myself, I managed to smile and what a smile it was. "LeeAnn! C'mon girl! It's time ta go! We gon be late and you know I on like being late!", voice yelled from another part of the house. Mrs. Smith was your grandmother and she had come by to pick us up for church that day. The pressure that lady put on me was indescribable. She came in fussing, "Girl if we waited on you, Jesus will don got to the church and gone and we miss the whole thang!" "I'm coming Momma Smith, I'm coming. I just wanna make sure we got everything we might need." "A baby don't need nothing but a pamper and a bottle. I tell ya you young mommas pack like ya going off for weeks. You know dem folks ain't gon be in church but an hour. Jesus don't get too much time outta them devils down 'er", she said sneeringly. Your granny reached and picked our shiny bundle of joy up. I

Soon to be Released Sneak Peek

can hear her saying, "Awwwwww, look at granny snoota woota! Him look just like he poppa! I remember when James was this age. He probably done shit his pamper too! His daddy always waited just as good as we got ready to go somewhere, then shit all over his self! Ain't that just like a man?" she said laughing, while she moved to begin situating you in your car-seat carrier for the ride. "Oh dear, where did I lay my ring?" I remember asking. What did I say that for? That lady got started and I didn't think she was going to ever stop. "What ring? You mean to tell me that no good son of mine had the nerve to give you a ring? And just what kind of ring is it supposed to be LeeAnn? I know it ain't supposed to be no engagement ring. James done lost his mind." I was so young and dumb back then that I said, "Well, I suppose it is my engagement ring Momma Smith. I don't know, but I love it. And I love him! I know he loves me" Ole mean heifer gon say, "I know you do baby. It's a fool born every minute and sometimes they fall in love." What kinda evil shit is that to say? Anyway, I didn't say nothing. Big Momma raised us to be respectful so that's what I did. I hesitated, thought about saying something, but I bit down on my tongue. Besides, my mind was more on finding the ring, than it was what Momma Smith was saying, plus I didn't want to offend her because I was hopelessly in love with her son. I was in love with that man, do you hear me? Your daddy was something else. He was about 14 years older than me and we met while I was in the city going to college. One of the work study programs in Natchez would connect students with older people in the area and allow them to earn money for school by running errands or cleaning for them. Momma Smith was one of the areas elderly participants that I got connected with, and we hit it off from the jump. I was over her house all the time, so

159

Soon to be Released Sneak Peek

it was only a matter of time before I met James. He was a charming older guy. I didn't know nothing about dating, I hadn't dated very many guys and had never even thought of having sex. Along came your daddy. Smooth talk, expensive watches, dress slacks, hat tilted to the side and always kept a little money in my pocket. He was easy to talk to and unusually considerate, thoughtful like I had never seen before. Without realizing, I was falling for him. We would sit up late talking, laying in the bed of his pick-up, staring up at the clear star-filled sky. He always called to see how my day at school was and find out if I needed anything. The main restaurants in the Natchez Mississippi area focused on seafood and I was allergic to seafood. Once James knew that, he made it a priority to go by the store and pick up foods that I wanted and sometimes he would even cook it and have it ready at his mom's house for me when I came by. Momma Smith would always say, "I thank James left something in there for you. If I ain't know better, I would thank my no-good son up to no good". Found my ring and boy was I giddy, slipping it on my finger. I didn't know what the day had in store for me at that moment, if I did, I would've stayed at the house. Adjusting our clothes, we both gave ourselves the final once-overs as they headed to the car. "Did you remember to cut the oven down? I sure would hate if them neckbones burn up while we up here call ourselves serving the Lord." I was so kiss ass polite, "Yes maam, I did. It's going to be fine. Thank you for stopping by and picking us up. I thought James was going to come by, but he called and said he wasn't feeling well." That wench knew something, now that I think about it. "Is that right? Hmph!" she grunted. The church they went to was only a few miles away, so it wasn't long before we was pulling up and I was waving at other members from the backseat window like I was in a presidential processional. I was sitting in the backseat with you. When we parked and got out, I hadn't even gotten Charles' carrier unstrapped fully when a strong voice said, "Good morning Sis. Gurthie. You look like heaven made you itself! Praise the Lord! Wonder how much praying I gotta do to get a good God-fearing woman like you? I bet you make the best banana pudding. Anyway, I can get a little taste of yo banana pudding", the man ask. "Brother Clark, if you don't get outta here with that talk ya ole devil! I came here to get Jesus ad you in the parking lot trying to make me sin! Hell nawl you can't taste my banana pudding. What kinda clown ass line is that anyway?" The man smiled then turned his full focus to me, I'm still wrestling with the straps on your carrier, it was one of those stupid Graco car-seat things. "And who pray tell is this tender blossom of beauty?" I was just a blushing but before I could answer, Momma Smith with a devilish smile and sassy head tilt answered, "That's LeeAnn. That's James lil girlfriend and their son Charles." "James? James Smith? Deacon James Smith? Ahhhhhh, I see. Nice to meet you young lady. So how long you and Deacon Smith been together?" "Get on inside and quit messing with that girl devil! She ain't gotta answer no questions for you" I'm still standing there clueless. "That's okay Momma Smith. We been in love since da beginning of last year." I answered like a big dummy. "I see. Well, it was nice seeing ya Sis. Gurthie. I'm sure I'll see you inside. Once again, sholl was a pleasure meeting ya young lady. Sholl is a handsome lil fella you and Deacon Smith got there" "Thank ya sir", I replied. Brother Clark walked hastily inside the slightly opened wood doors and you could hear the choir singing coming from inside the church. Momma Smith walked into the sanctuary and as the ushers that kept the door smiled and greeted her, they looked at me with the eyes of amazement. I could sense the tension and hostility brewing but I chalked it up as visitor stiffness. When I walked between the two ladies I kinda glanced back casually. In my peripheral, I could see the one lean over and whisper something sneakily to the other. We were directed to the back-right side of the congregation to seats about four rows from the very last pew. Before I made it over to the seat, I gazed across the sanctuary and found Mr. Clark, the gentleman we had just met outside. He was sitting on the second row from the front, the side opposite where we were headed to. He was leaning forward with both hands on the shoulder of a man that looked just like your daddy. Before I could adjust the look of bewilderment on my face, a voice cried out from the choir stand. "Awwwwww hell nawl! This bitch done come up in here!" The woman was furiously trying to get down from her place in the choir stand and appeared to be referring to me. I'm standing there clueless. The lady was emotionally undone and screaming repeated threats. "Ima kill her! Ima kill dat bitch today! Nawl. Lord nawl!" The pastor was on his feet attempting to get control, repeatedly calling her name over the microphone. "Sis. Smith. Sis. Smith", he said. "Sis. Smith?", I said in my head. By then, yo jive ass daddy had rushed to the head the woman off and prevent her from getting around the crowd to where I was. "Baby calm down. Calm down baby, let me explain." "Explain? How the hell you explain this James Earl? Ima kill her! Let me go! Let me go!" "Baby?", I'm asking myself quietly, tears falling from my eyes. The whole church was in a state of confusion while Momma Smith sat quietly looking with a shady smirk. "James? James, you're married?", I ask him from across the room. "Yes, bitch he is married!

Soon to be Released Sneak Peek

Sholl is! What's yo next move now bitch? He been married and I been knew about yo whorish ass! You must be out yo damn mind! You gon die today bitch! Get out my way", she huffed still scuffling to get closer to me. I was broken half in two. I gasped with a sigh of disbelief and almost immediately caught eyes with a young boy sitting close by where your daddy was sitting. The boy couldn't have been more than two years old, but he was crying "Momma. Stop screaming mooooomma." Two other boys sat on each side of the crying two-year old and they all resembled James too much for me to not put two and two together. Charles interrupted his momma at this point, "Are you telling me my daddy was married. Married with two kids?" Three kids boy. Pay attention and don't interrupt me, let me finish. All over the church, members were crying, shaking their heads, some looking at me with the face of loathsome disgust, others walking out altogether. I felt so yucky. Lied to and used. The church members were staring at me like I had done some evil thing, but son all I did was believe what a charming man told me. I had no idea he was married. So here I was, still doing all I could to gather my thoughts, standing there numb to what was happening, a gentleman walked up and said in a quieted but firm tone, "ma'am, I think it's going to best if you and yo baby leave". Taking a few more breaths, staring at the man I loved with all my being across this hallowed place, comforting his wife, I chucked that ring across the sanctuary. "LIAR!", I remember screaming. "Get to hell bitch!" Mrs. Smith shouted. I grabbed you right then son and headed for the door. I gave one last look back and the wife said, "Wait! Is that? James is that yo baby? James that bet not be yo baby!", she shrieked. I walked out. I walked fast, my sweaty fat ass stumbling through the grass on the side of the dirt road,

163

Soon to be Released Sneak Peek

hoping I was headed in the right direction. I felt all the pain of life in that moment. The first man I trusted and gave myself to, the first man I had loved, the father of my firstborn son was married with children. Every reality of what my life was about to be had been choked. Mangled and murdered by the deceitful betrayal of the person I loved with all my heart. Tears wet my plump round face, just after I reached down to take those troublesome heels off that your daddy bought by the way, I heard a voice say "Maam? Young lady? I be happy to give you a lift. Nearest road bout 2 miles down and if I ain't mistaken, you need to be headed back the other ways." I was so mad, I kept stomping away like I didn't hear the man. Thank about it now, surprised I didn't fling you out that carrier the ways I was swanging that thing. "Maam? I'm sholl sorry bout what happened back there. You ain't have no ways of knowing." I turned to see the face of the man speaking to find out it was Bro. Clark. His questions and bewildered look made more sense to me at that point, so I ask him, "Why didn't you tell me then Bro. Clark? You knew when you saw me getting out that car, I was about to go in there and have my whole world fall apart!" "Naw now, I ain't had no ways of knowing what would or wouldn't happen. Plus, I was just as shocked to see you as anybody else in that building. Telling you wasn't my place, that's James Earl business. C'mon let me give you a ride. It's the least I can do." I paused, thought to myself for a minute. The way my feet was throbbing and the fact I had no clue where I was going, sure helped in me in making the decision. I waddled my chunky, pouting ass around the front of the car to climb in the back-passenger seat. "Now. Where you like to go?" "Home" I told him, "I just wanna go home". "Where's

Soon to be Released Sneak Peek

home?" "Jackson. Jackson Mississippi." "Alrighty then", Bro. Clark smiled and said, "let's getcha home".

Soon to be Released Sneak Peek

"Evolution"

Forgiveness:

It was never my intention to write a book and even after years of encouragement from my wife, it still was not my intention to write a book to help someone gain momentum in life. I always considered myself more of a poet for the most part and would've been completely content with just writing that. Once I finished my first book of poetry, I was proofreading it for mistakes and making changes when I became sad and discouraged. The words were painful, and every line was filled with resentment and shame. The book title was going to be *Poetically Undone* and the writing was indeed a true reflection of the author's disposition. Just to give you an idea of what I mean, here's a couple of the poems from the book:

Brokenness created insecurity.
Hurt came from demonic voices
inside that kept luring me.
I chose to follow my own choices.

The shame of what has passed,
the discomfort of what's to come,
the disappointment of what is now living

Soon to be Released Sneak Peek

in the deeds of what's been done.

There is no brokenness in me!
There are no demons, only me.
Filled with unbelief and issues
I never took time to see

A significant number of poems I wrote were directed toward a painful period in my childhood and the words lashed out at the parents that I have always held responsible for that pain. When I was writing it felt liberating to finally just say how it made me feel and get it off my chest. After all, who doesn't like to tell how they feel? The feelings are real, the pain is inescapable, and the reality of the consequential behavior produced considering the experience can usually haunt an individual all their God given life unless the do something about it. No, I don't mean get the person back that committed the offense towards you although that is becoming the more popular reaction across the globe. An article from Greater Good Magazine titled *Which Feels Better, Forgiveness or Revenge,* shared the results of a study on bullying done at Macquarie University in Australia. They took 135 students that had been the victims of bullying in the past 6 months, led them through a psychological test that caused them to relive the incident in their minds while the audio played. Afterwards the students were given a survey to answer some questions about their thoughts and feelings concerning the bullying experience. The following phase

Soon to be Released Sneak Peek

of the study split the students into three groups and gave each group a separate audio influence to lead them through a particular response. One group was to respond with avoidance, the other with forgiveness and the third with revenge. Of course, on paper the young people would agree that revenge is the most appropriate way to deal with the bully but the study and the readings in vitals discovered that while the forgiveness and avoidance group initially spiked at the idea of dealing with the bully this way, as they were coached to imagine themselves forgiving the bully, they calmed down significantly. The revenge group did not have the self-empowering self-esteem feelings that the facilitators anticipated. They were surprised because instead of a rise in the sense of self-esteem, it went down. Imagine that, you finally get the chance to get that mean ole bully back and it makes you feel worse than you felt before. Why? Because you cannot overcome evil with evil. Only with good can evil be overthrown. Only with forgiveness is a man or woman ever able to move forward and shake themselves free of hurtful places they relive over and over. Like I was explaining, most of the poetry in the poetry book I compiled worse echoing with the chants of a broken and hurtful past. Rather than sharing the wonderful things about my life, my health, my wife and kids, I was belly aching and wallowing in the old "my daddy wasn't there for me" stories. Every tree in America could give its life to make paper and it still would not be enough to hold inscriptions of pain that we all could fill the pages up with. I dated a young lady one time and she would share stories with me of how her

Soon to be Released Sneak Peek

dad's close friend, who was reverenced by them as their uncle, had molested her from the time she was 12. She's 48 now and still carrying that pain. Another close female friend was encouraged by her mom to have an abortion when she became pregnant with her first child. Of course, we like to think that mother knows best, but she's 42 now and still feels the resentment towards her mother. Close friend of mine has never really pulled himself out of the place of challenging questions when he contemplates why God would take his daddy from him at the age of two, leaving him to face life as an uncertain, lonely male. He's 45 now. I have a relative that resents her mom because the mom during her younger years was pursuing a college degree and decidedly left her daughter with the grandmother. While in the care of the grandmother, the young girl, then 3 years old, was molested by an older male that was not closely associated with the family. Then yours truly, the son of an extra marital affair that left both parents regretting the decision they had made and the result of that decision, me. The question my entire life was "why don't my parents love me?". Nobody ever took time to answer that question at all but over the years, I developed a resentment to help me deal with the pain I felt. It seemed more appropriate to situate a deep-seated grudge, rather than keep some bright-eyed hope of happily ever after where one of them, either one of them, decided I was important. I had to be tough. I had to muster up strength to go on. Instead of strength, all I did was harbor the hurt of unforgiveness and every time I would write anything in the form of poetry, it showed.

Soon to be Released Sneak Peek

Every time I attempted to exist inside a loving relationship, it showed up. Anytime I disagreed with something my mother would say, y internal reaction pointed to the fact that I had not forgiven her and that place of pain in my life was still in control, not me. An African Proverb says, "When there is no enemy within, the enemy without can do us no harm". I always thought that referred primarily to the things inside us that fight against us daily. Our lust and unchecked emotional frustrations. That would mean it to be interpreted, if we have conquered the enemy inside us, our external enemies cannot prevail. Makes perfect sense to me, until I was reminded that I have enemies inside of me so it's impossible for me to see clearly. The reasoning, even at its best, will not allow us to negate the presence and power of perception. Perception being the mental interpretation of what you see. So, what did I see? I saw enemies within me. The enemies I saw were my parents and to keep them held captive as enemies, I had to continually relive a childhood that I wanted nothing more than to forget. The Apostle Paul in 2 Corinthians chapter 10 wrote:

"3For though we walk in the flesh, we do not war after the flesh: 4(For the weapons of our warfare are not carnal, but mighty through God to the pulling down of STRONG HOLDS;) 5Casting down IMAGINATIONSs, and every high thing that exalteth itself against the knowledge of God".

Soon to be Released Sneak Peek

We may read by that in passing but it takes on new meaning when you recognize a stronghold in your own life. A stronghold is something that has a stronghold on you. It keeps you held in a place, unable to move and hopelessly surrender to the incarcerated thinking of that situation. Things would cross my mind(imaginations) and I would be taken back mentally to a space in time (the stronghold) where I felt the most pain of my life. The insanity of it is that even when I put forth effort to live as the man I am today, I could not live life apart from the boy I was then because I was holding onto him. Launching an exciting writing career and taking off as a public speaker, but almost every word written or spoken was and expression of that place. I could not be who I was designed to be now because I was help by the emotional grip of who I was then. My mom could not be the mother to me that she wanted to be now because my perception made her an enemy within. If there is no enemy within, the enemy without can do us no harm. The reason the enemy cannot do us any harm without is because they're no longer an enemy. Jesus told us to love our enemies, pray for those that intend to misuse us. The only way they are no longer enemies is because you have forgiven them.

A very good friend of mine ask me once a long time ago what was the one cause for divorce? He had just finished preaching a sermon on marriage and I was quizzing him for more learning because at that time, my marriage was going through the westside of hell and turning on calamity boulevard. We would try to make it to church but one Sunday morning we were fighting

Soon to be Released Sneak Peek

right before church and because it was such a small
assembly, everybody could tell. We sat on different rows
and the more I watched my wife, the angrier I became.
This Sunday morning happened to be one of our more
civil Sundays and we both sat attentively in our most
holy posture. He spoke and informed us one how we
were supposed to treat each other and stay together
forever but he didn't tell us how to move past the
temptation to kill each other. I waited, I listened, I
prayed, still no luck. I heard the same thing I always
heard about marriage, just stay in there and tough it out.
When he finished, we stood there laughing and talking in
a small men's circle and he asked that golden question,
"do you know what the one cause of divorce is?". Me,
being the know-it-all that I am immediately replied
"money". "Nope", he replied with a smirking I-Know-
the-answer kind of grin. "Infidelity?" "Nope!" "Kids?"
"No." "You give up?", he asked the group and I was the
first one to say YES. "Unforgiveness", he answered. We
all stood there bewildered as humanly possible because
that didn't even seem like something that should have
been in the running, but he postured himself to teach. "A
marriage is a relationship between two great forgivers."
When Jesus spoke to the crowd that questioned him
about divorce and wondered about Moses writing a
certificate of divorce, he told them, Moses because of the
hardness of your hearts was permitted to write a
certificate of divorce, but from the beginning it was not
so. When the heart is hard, it does not seek to forgive
and will never choose to forgive. It's like the statement
"I can never get over what they did to me!". Of course,

you can't because you've made a hard place in your heart that states you never can. When we went to church and I held a bitter place in my heart towards my wife, I made my heart hard. I made her an enemy inside my mind. She could not be anything else to me because of what I had determined her to be within. How can anyone get along with someone that has decided who they were before they have a chance to be anything else? You can't. Not only are you making them an enemy in your mind, holding them captive, you yourself are being held captive by that stronghold and will never move to any other place until you forgive them.

This book replaced the poetry book for the simple fact that it was not necessary to make my parents feel pain in order to move past that place of hurt. These feelings were mine to deal with and mine to resolve. Writing them out did help me detail exactly what I was feeling but it was not a book for the sake of publishing after all. No, the truth of it all is that for you or me to have a fulfilling life of bountiful destiny and exponential love, we must forgive people we hold grudgingly in our hearts. Most people bought this book as self-help and therapy. Some bought it for the sake of motivating them to a productive place of business. Others know that this book has been helpful to countless numbers of married couples in their efforts to rebuild and maintain healthy levels of intimacy and understanding. Regardless the reason for getting and reading this book, no matter what area of life you choose to apply the learning, this lesson must be common to all and in all. A human heart that harbors unforgiveness is stifling growth and constricting the channels of creativity, rendering them ineffective. Unforgiveness is like a clogged AC filter in the central air conditioning units of the home. It's not the only thing that can clog it, but it will leave it just as dirty as any other shortcoming we discover in life. Much like the AC unit and its filter, the air is cold, and the unit still works, but it's having to pull harder because the flow is restricted. The filter must be replaced. A new one must be put in with no debris or impurities. King David ask that God would create in him a clean heart and renew a right spirit within him. That's what has to happen in order to function productively and effectively in any aspect of life, business and relationship. The debris must be removed and the people that are being held bound as enemies in our mind, must be set free. Out of everything you read in these pages, this is by far the most important, the most revolutionizing, and the absolute hardest. The last thing I would even attempt to do is coax you into believing that forgiving someone is easy. We're talking about years and years of hurts in some cases. We're talking ex-husbands and ex-wives that may have done some of the most unimaginably unkind things to one another after explaining they would love and care for them until death do them apart. We're talking revisiting the very thing you have wanted all your life to run away from. It is the death that no man or woman wants to die. It relinquishes pride and dethrones all pride filled personality, but it must happen. It must happen for you, and it must happen for them. Before you go one to the next chapter, find the places of unforgiveness in your heart. Find them, pray over those places and release the people associated with it altogether. Continue to pray and release them until the tears flow and then release them even more. It's time. You've held onto it long enough. Forgive whoever you need to forgive so you can get on with life and life more abundantly.

Acknowledgements

My conscience and integrity would not allow me to come to the end of this project and not pay homage to the Most High God of Abraham, Isaac and Jacob for allowing me to venture into such an endeavor as this. It has been encouraging, it challenged me to complete what I started, and it helped me look to Him for the things I never believed could be done. Immediately following my appreciation to God, I must thank this amazing portion of divine femininity I have beside me, behind me and out front pulling me at times to ensure I don't give up or give in. The daughter of Zion, the Diadem of our dwelling, our Queen. Without her support and constant encouragement of redirection, I never would've typed the first word. She has believed in me from the moment we said, "I do". We laughed, chided, mourned and prayed about this project. It brought us closer, into a deeper, more purposeful relationship with God and each other. She stood by me and admittedly, stood for me at times. I applaud her as a woman and cherish her as a wife, mother and friend. Florida Miller, I salute you soldier. Keekee? My sister. Even more than that at times, but I cannot leave her name off this publication. She proofread

176

Acknowledgements

work, called me into accountability and at times, fussed, but she was there. Means the world to have people there when you're attempting things, you're uncertain about. Steadfast, dependable, caring people that will not give up on you and will not let you give up. They make sure it gets done. Shaun, Anton, Miguel and Duanne Lloyd….these brothers were constant sounding boards. They were like the stone walls I could slam the tennis ball of frustration against when life was too hard. They are strong men, families of their own and lives that demand balance, focus and constant attention; but they all have been a phone call away and not one day has passed where one of them was not in my ear. Shay Jackson has been a wealth of knowledge and willingly answering questions to ensure the product meets standard and timelines. Phonecia Wilson, her admonition in troubling moments of indecisiveness. Love you my sister. Countless numbers of loved ones, my Nikki, Niambi, and DJ. The greatest teacher in all the Westcoast, Leticia Cortez…we did it Lety! DK and Dulum for spiritual reinforcement and correction when needed, much needed, much appreciated. Cool B for his talent and contribution to the arts.(Keep it up Cool, I believe in you brother. Go Hard!) An

Acknowledgements

endless list of friends and enemies inspired the words in this compilation over several years, too many to name one by one. My Bird for telling me right out of love and always being there when I call; Team Miller owes you bigtime. I must pay my respect to My Shady Oaks family! We the best! We do what we do and represent each other in whatever way possible. No matter where we are in the world, I am who I am because of the lives we lived together right there in Shady Oaks Mississippi. It's 4 Life! Shady Oaks 4 Life. The Queens, the nieces and nephews. Finally, I thank each of you. That purchased this book, that read this book and that allowed the words inscribed quantify clear pictures of emotions and experience. I could not love you more. Until we meet again.... C. Miller

Mrs. Miller...We did it Baby!!!

Made in the
USA
Columbia, SC

78663570R00107